Dogs & Society:

Anglo-American Sociological Perspectives

(1865-1934)

Harriet Martineau
Charles Darwin
Frances Power Cobbe
Roscoe Pound
Charlotte Perkins Gilman
Annie Marion MacLean
George Herbert Mead

Edited by

MICHAEL R. HILL

and

MARY JO DEEGAN

Copyright 2016 by Michael R. Hill and Mary Jo Deegan

ISBN 978-1-60962-096-7 paperback

Zea Books are published by the University of Nebraska–Lincoln Libraries
Electronic (pdf) edition available online at http://digitalcommons.unl.edu
Print edition available from http://www.lulu.com/spotlight/unlib

UNIVERSITY OF
Nebraska
Lincoln®

Contents

List of Figures in Chapter 3

Preface

We are indebted to Giuseppina Cersosimo and Raffaele Rauty who, intrigued by the special issue on dogs in *Sociological Origins*,[1] encouraged us to prepare this work as a separately published volume, translated into Italian,[2] and now made available in the original English. We are grateful to Dr. Paul Royster for his interest and expertise in bringing this version to the light of day via Zea, the digital publishing initiative of the UNL Libraries. We thank the University of Chicago Press for permission to reprint excerpts from George Herbert Mead's *Mind Self & Society*. We are grateful also to *Sociological Origins* for permission to reprint portions of the materials appearing in the 2003 symposium issue on dogs. We sincerely hope this volume proves to be an interesting thematic reader/resource for students enrolled in theory/history courses in classical sociology.

This book is dedicated to
Dr. Anne L. Cepela, veterinarian *extraordinaire*.

---

[1] *Sociological Origins*, Vol 3, No 1 (Autumn), 2003. Special Issue: Symposium on Dogs, Society and Sociologists.

[2] *Cani & Società: Prospettive sociologiche anglo-americane 1865-1925*, edited and introduced by Michael R. Hill and Mary Jo Deegan. Translated and with an afterword (postfazioni) by Raffaele Rauty. Esplorazioni No. 20. (A sociological series edited by Giuseppina Cersosimo). Calimera (Italy): Edizioni Kurumuny, 2014.

The senior editor's father, Raymond Hilligoss, Jr.,
circa 1915

1

Dogs and Society: A Sociological Introduction

Michael R. Hill and Mary Jo Deegan

H UMANS AND DOGS have a long, wonderful and sometimes problematic association. At a personal level, dogs have been integral to our lives, and our parents' lives, for as long as the two of us can remember. As sociologists, we also recognize that dogs are important at the macro level. Here, we introduce a selection of early sociological arguments about dogs and their social relationships with humankind. Our interest in developing this book began when we encountered the delightful essays on dogs by Charlotte Perkins Gilman and Annie Marion MacLean — two insightful Anglo-American sociologists who present opposing sympathies regarding the canine world. Admirers and detractors of dogs reflect important sensibilities within Anglo-American society. This book is a smorgasbord of sociological standpoints, all written by some of sociology's most perceptive practitioners, from 1865 to 1934. We are delighted with the opportunity to make these essays more widely available.

As these readings document, dogs are intrinsically social beings. Likewise, our observations of dogs, our interactions with dogs, and our writings about dogs are markedly social phenomena. Dogs are not only part of our social world, they also inform our sociological imagination at both micro and macro levels.

At the micro level, we are informed by the social psychological aspects of dog/human and dog/dog relationships. Unstated biases and anthropocentric presumptions surface quickly and instructively when sociologists attend seriously and reflexively to other animal species. For example, Leslie Irvine[1] recently explored the mistakes made by George Herbert Mead in failing to "listen" to his dog. The extreme phenomenological bracketing required to "understand" what it might be like to "think like a dog" helps us to reframe our conceptions of "the other" in dramatic and instructive ways. One benefit of thinking earnestly in terms of other animal species is to lead us to less anthropocentric conceptions of sociology as a whole.

---

[1] L. Irvine, "George's Bulldog: What Mead's Canine Companion Could Have Told Him about the Self," *Sociological Origins* 3 (Autumn 2003: 46-49); *If You Tame Me: Understanding Our Connection with Animals* (Temple University Press, 2004).

1

At the macro level, the incorporation of dogs within human institutional patterns is no small matter. Relevant topics ripe for continuing investigation include: the organization and activities of kennel clubs (eg., The American Kennel Club, the Ente Nazionale della Cinofilia Italiana, etc.); occupations for dogs (including herding, police work, and seeing-eye, hearing, signal, and other service duties); societies for the prevention of cruelty to animals and animal rights movements (eg., Humane Society International); the social economics of pet care (including purchase, maintenance, veterinary services, and the like); the legal and health status of dogs and dog owners, the human benefits of dog companionship, and the intricacies of dog-related social problems in urban and rural areas; and, more widely, the place of dogs in one's culture overall, to include literature, art, religion, humor, and so on.

Sociological considerations of dogs are not new, as the pioneering selections in this book demonstrate. Nonetheless, advocates for official recognition of such analyses within the American Sociological Association (ASA) met, until recently, with stiff resistance. David Nibert[2] documented the institutional arrogance and anthropocentrism exhibited by ASA officers in his account of the origins of the newly-formed ASA Section on Animals & Society. In opposing the formation of the Section, the members of earlier ASA Councils demonstrated that many influential sociologists too frequently see "politics" and "unscientific motives" everywhere but in their own donnish agendas.

Academic and scholarly politics aside, animals generally — and dogs in particular — pose sober sociological questions. For starters: somewhat more than 70 million dogs are kept as pets in the USA alone.[3] The *National Geographic News* calculated for 2010 that there were 500 million dogs worldwide, many of which were free roaming.[4] The social consequences of these large numbers can be dramatic. In economic terms alone, sales for all pet foods in the U.S. for 2015 stood at 23 billion dollars.[5] Practically speaking, most people like dogs while some others fear them. Whatever our experience with dogs, our emotional attachment is rarely neutral. This

---

[2] D. Nibert, "Origins of the ASA Section on Animals & Society: With a Bibliographic Appendix," *Sociological Origins* 3 (Autumn 2003: 53-58).

[3] American Veterinary Medical Association, *U.S. Pet Ownership & Demographics Sourcebook* (2012). Estimates for 2015 place the number at nearly 78 million dogs in the U.S. (American Pet Products Association, *2015-2016 APPA National Pet Owners Survey*).

[4] *National Geographic News*, October 28, 2010.

[5] American Pet Products Association, *2015-2016 APPA National Pet Owners Survey.*

outcome makes the topic of dogs inherently engaging and thereby opens the pedagogical door for sociological instruction, reflection, and debate.

We invite you now to return with us to our sociological foundations, to the vigor and originality exhibited by the authors in this book. The solutions, reflections, and rejoinders presented by these early writers exhibit intellectual verve, unflinching insight, and (usually) gracious good humor. As editors, we hope that you are both inspired and entertained by these selections.

A brief comment about the organization of this volume: The writings are presented in chronological order, and we provide a brief biographical introduction to each author at the head of his/her first appearance in the book. We have retained British and American spellings as they appeared in the original publications.

———————————

2

Dogs: Unauthorized, Unclaimed, and Vagabond [1]

(1865)
Harriet Martineau

Harriet Martineau (1802-1876), born in England, is widely regarded as the first female sociologist and, increasingly, as a founder of the discipline. She was an enormously prolific author.[2] Her circle of friends included the leading lights of Victorian England, including Erasmus Darwin, the elder brother of Charles Darwin. Martineau's major works include: *Illustrations of Political Economy* (1832-34), *Miscellanies* (1837), *Society in America* (1837), *Retrospect of Western Travel* (1838), *How to Observe Morals and Manners* (1838), *Life in the Sick-Room* (1844), *Eastern Life* (1848), *Household Education* (1849), *Letters from Ireland* (1852), the translation of Auguste Comte's *Positive Philosophy* (1853), *England and Her Soldiers* (1859), *Health, Husbandry and Handicraft* (1861), and her *Autobiography* (1877). Several thematic collections and new editions of Martineau's works have appeared recently. Various sociologists and myriad literary critics have written about Martineau in recent years.[3] Major sources

---

[1] Edited from the (London) *Daily News* May 19, 1865. For attribution of this originally untitled and unsigned "leader," see: E.S. Arbuckle, *Harriet Martineau in the London Daily News* (Garland, 1994: Appendix).

[2] Cf., J.B. Rivlin, *Harriet Martineau: A Bibliography of Her Separately Printed Books* (New York Public Library, 1947); Arbuckle, *op. cit.*, and D.A. Logan, *Further Letters* (Lehigh University Press, 2012: 585-91).

[3] E.g., M.R. Hill, "Empiricism and Reason in Harriet Martineau's Sociology," in Martineau's *How to Observe Morals and Manners*, sesquicentennial edition (Transaction, 1989: xv-lx); M.R. Hill, "Harriet Martineau," in *Women in Sociology*, ed. by M.J. Deegan (Greenwood, 1991: 289-97); S. Hoecker-Drysdale, *Harriet Martineau: First Woman Sociologist* (Birg, 1992); *Harriet Martineau:*

of intellectual and biographical data include *The Collected Letters of Harriet Martineau* (2007) and *Further Letters* (2012), both edited by Deborah Logan. The primary deposit of Harriet Martineau's papers is at the University of Birmingham Special Collections, much of which is microfilmed.[4]

IT IS SAID that in cities one half of the inhabitants does not know how the other lives; and it really seems, judging from the laughter which greeted the early speeches in the House of Commons on the Bill to restrain the ravage of flocks by dogs, as if, on the larger scale of the whole country, one half the people do not know how the other half grieves, chafes, or rejoices. Townspeople and political gentlemen are aware, in a superficial way, that there are periodical complaints of the unclaimed dogs that show themselves in our cities. The question comes up every summer how many owners of dogs evade paying the duty; and when the answer is that there are tens of thousands of nonpaying owners, there arises a cry for the destruction of such unauthorised dogs before the hot weather is upon us. At intervals a coroner's jury returns a verdict — as happened last week — of "Death from hydrophobia" of some poor child, or working man, or other person who does not wear boots or gloves, having been seized upon and bitten by a strange dog in the streets. Such complaints and catastrophes are not received with a laugh, like Sir F. Heygate's account of the

---

Theoretical and Methodological Perspectives, ed. by M.R. Hill and S. Hoecker-Drysdale (Routledge, 2001); M.R. Hill, "An Introduction to Harriet Martineau's Lake District Writings," in *An Independent Woman's Lake District Writings* (Humanity Books, 2004: 25-54); M.J. Deegan, "Harriet Martineau and the Sociology of Health," in *Advancing Gender Research from the Nineteenth to the Twenty-First Centuries*, ed. by M.T. Segal and V. Demos (Emerald, 2008: 43-61); B. Conway and M.R. Hill, "Harriet Martineau and Ireland," in *Social Thought on Ireland in the Nineteenth Century*, ed. by S. Ó Síocháin (University College Dublin Press, 2009: 47-66); M.R. Hill, "Harriet Martineau: The Founding and Refounding of Sociology," in *Harriet Martineau and the Birth of Disciplines*, edited by Valerie Sanders and Gaby Weiner (Routledge, 2016). An outstanding literary analysis is Deb Logan's *The Hour and the Woman: Harriet Martineau's "Somewhat Remarkable" Life* (Northern Illinois University Press, 2002).

[4] For discussion of additional acquisitions, see: C. Penney, "Beyond the Microfilm: Harriet Martineau and the University of Birmingham Special Collections," *Sociological Origins* 3 (Spring, 2005: 69-70).

doings of the dogs in Ireland;[5] but the nuisance in London and other towns is not to be compared for a moment with that which has been endured till now in Ireland, and in some parts of England and Scotland.

When we read history we feel as if it must have been a fearful thing to live in the days of wolves; and we follow with interest the offers of royal rewards for wolves' heads, and note down in our memories the date of the last head money paid for the wolf. We sympathise with the flockmaster in Australia, who has to carry on a perpetual warfare with the dingo — the native dog, of a satanic aspect and temper — which is the plague of Australian pastoral life. It worries draught animals, and devours sheep and poultry, and half ruins many a settler. Our countrymen who have travelled in Egypt, or have frequented Asiatic cities, have very grave impressions of the prowling dogs which abound there, and are truly almost as formidable as the wild beasts of the desert and the jungle. Discountenanced by Mohammedan law, like pigs, they are no man's property, and under no man's charge; and they may therefore well be enemies of man. While sensible of such nuisances as these, and ready to pity the people who are subject to them, we have actually had no sympathy and compassion ready for the sufferers from wild dogs in our own islands; and when it is stated that one cannot go anywhere in Ireland without being beset by dogs, the House laughs, heedless of what such a fact implies.

The emigration from Ireland has turned loose hundreds of thousands of dogs to become wild. One member reckons the Irish dogs at a million; another at a million and a half; and Sir R. Peel at two millions.[6] These vagrant dogs worry sheep, and cattle, and pigs, communicate vermin to them, spoil their health and their repose, hinder their fattening, and kill off the sheep by thousands in a year. The sheep killed outright and reported to the police were 6,147 in 1864; and in an incalculable number of cases the police are not appealed to at all — so small have hitherto been the chances of redress. One terrible feature of the case is the progressive increase of fatal cases of hydrophobia in Ireland, as we learn from Professor Gamgee.[7] For the ten

---

[5] Frederick William Heygate (1822-1894) quipped during parliamentary discussion in May, 1865, that "there were 900,000 inhabited houses in Ireland, and that it was very probable that there was on the whole a dog to each house."

[6] Robert Peel (1822-1895), 3rd Baronet, was an English politician. His father, of the same name, was Prime Minister of England.

[7] John Gamgee (1841-1909), physician; see: J. Gamgee, "Prevalence and Prevention of Diseases amongst Domestic Animals of Ireland," *Dublin Quarterly Journal of Science* 3 (1863): 89-107. See also: N. Pemberton and M. Worboys, *Mad Dogs and Englishmen: Rabies in Britain, 1930-2000* (Palgrave Macmillan, 2007).

6

years ending in 1841 there were 31 cases reported; in the next ten years 57 cases; and in the ten ending in 1861, 61. This was while the fatal cases in Scotland were too few to afford material for an average; and while in England they had declined from 25 to 3 in the latter ten years. In County Down, it appears, the farmers had left off keeping sheep at all — so great were their losses from dogs. In Donegal 1,410 sheep were so destroyed last year; and in only 449 instances in the six thousand and odd were the owners of the dogs ascertained, and made to pay damages. It is a very serious matter that now, when wool and mutton are in unprecedented request, and the rural fortunes of Ireland so sorely need amending, a mischief like this should be abroad — wasting the flocks, depraving the wool and the mutton by vermin and disease, exasperating the grazier, and ruining the small farmer. It was time that the Government should take in hand an evil which the occupiers of farms could not deal with individually.

Martineau and her pet cat.

But it was not only of Ireland that such disagreeable stories were told. Mr. Fenwick,[8] on occasion of the second reading of his Bill, declared his belief that farmers in every county in England could complain of losses of sheep from strange dogs; and from his own county there was a return of no less than 962 cases, in no one of which had any compensation been obtained, because the sufferers could not prove that the aggressive dogs were in the habit of worrying sheep, and were known by their owners to be so. It is not surprising that, in such a state of affairs, the Grand Jury of the county, the Poor-law Guardians, the Highway authorities, and Agricultural Societies, have petitioned Parliament in favour of such a reform as is hoped from the new Bill. In the United States, in France, in Belgium, and other countries, live stock and human life and limb are protected by law from this particular injury; and if some things that happen in remote or scantily peopled

---

[8] Henry Fenwick (1820-1868).

districts of our country were known, there could be no doubt of the necessity of a legislative Act such as has now passed.[9] In some of the agricultural counties law and right are popularly understood in regard to all appropriate offences, as factory law and right are popularly understood in Yorkshire and Lancashire. In the eastern counties, the humblest rustic goes with his shilling in his hand for the trespass if his donkey has got into a neighbour's field through carelessness about the gate; while in the hill districts, where the old-fashioned inhabitants have no notions, or wrong ones, about law and right, a flock of wild and ravening sheep in March may devastate a market garden, or cattle may rove and eat off the whole root crop of a neighbour, and the owner of the stock will never imagine such a thing as making reparation. He gives liberally in charity, but compensation for injury he will not hear of. He calls it a bad job, and says it can't be helped now. If his own beasts are worried, he frets or takes it easily according to his constitution; but he does not set about getting reparation. If his dogs have done the mischief to a neighbour, he takes no notice of any summons to pay or justify himself; he cannot believe that anything can come of it, that anybody can hurt *him*; and if the case is brought into court he has taken no steps towards a defence. If he is worated[10] and has to pay, he is heartbroken, thinks all the world has gone against him, and too probably taken refuge in drink, and goes to ruin. These are the sort of people who let their own bullocks get bogged, and their sheep snowed up, and their lambs pinched with frost, and their poultry carried off by foxes and hawks — the sort of men to give up keeping sheep on account of the wild dogs, instead of calling on the police and the neighbourhood to help to get rid of the nuisance. The new Act may put fresh spirit into apathetic men, as well as console and encourage the more enterprising; it will compel the owners of dogs to see after them, to claim them, to be responsible for them, and pay damages for mischief done; and it will go a long way towards separating the owned from the vagabond dogs, and towards securing a good clearance of the latter. If the new Act does not do this, we must try again.

---

[9] Dogs Act 1865 (later replaced by the Dogs Act of 1903).

[10] For the English word "worated," The *Oxford English Dictionary* provides no clear model or definition; this instance is possibly a typographical error, a corruption of "worried" (in the sense of pestered or harassed), an obsolete variant of "warranted" (in the sense of compelled or directed by an authority to perform a duty), or a rare parochial English expression.

Chapter 3

The Expression of the Emotions in Dogs [1]
(1872)

Charles Darwin

Charles Darwin (1809-1882) was the extraordinary English naturalist whose *Origin of Species* (1859) provided the foundation for all subsequent discussions of biological and social evolution. His later work, *The Expression of the Emotions in Man and Animals* (1872) is an important source for students of nonverbal communication, symbolic interaction and "conversations of gestures." The literature on Darwin is so enormous and well known that little need be said here.[2] It bears mention, however, that Charles' older brother, Erasmus (1804-1881), was a close friend of Harriet Martineau. The major deposit of Charles Darwin's archival papers is at Cambridge University Library. Large portions of this material have been digitized and are available online via the Complete Works of Charles Darwin Online and the Darwin Correspondence Project.

_____

WHEN A DOG approaches a strange dog or man in a savage or hostile frame of mind he walks upright and very stiffly; his head is slightly raised, or not much lowered; the tail is held erect, and quite rigid; the hairs bristle, especially along the neck and back; the pricked ears are directed forwards, and the eyes have a fixed stare: (see Figures 1 and 2). These actions, as will hereafter be

_____

[1] Edited from Charles Darwin, *The Expression of the Emotions in Man and Animals*, New York: D. Appleton, 1898 (First published 1872). Note: the figures have been re-ordered and renumbered.

[2] For a succinct biographical sketch, see: Frank H. Hankins, "Darwin, Charles Robert (1809-82)," *Encyclopaedia of the Social Sciences*, vol. 5, edited by E.R.A. Seligman and A. Johnson (New York: Macmillan, 1931: 4-5).

explained, follow from the dog's intention to attack his enemy, and are thus to a large extent intelligible. As he prepares to spring with a savage growl on his enemy, the canine teeth are uncovered, and the ears are pressed close backwards on the head; but with these latter actions, we are not here concerned. Let us now suppose that the dog suddenly discovers that the man he is approaching, is not a stranger, but his master; and let it be observed how completely and instantaneously his whole bearing is reversed. Instead of walking upright, the body sinks downwards or even crouches,

Figure 1

and is thrown into flexuous movements; his tail, instead of being held stiff and upright, is lowered and wagged from side to side; his hair instantly becomes smooth; his ears are depressed and drawn backwards, but not closely to the head; and his lips hang loosely. From the drawing back of the ears, the eyelids become elongated, and the eyes no longer appear round and staring. It should be added that the animal is at such times in an excited condition from joy; and nerve-force will be generated in excess, which naturally leads to action of some kind. Not one of the above

10

movements, so clearly expressive of affection, are of the least direct service to the animal. They are explicable, as far as I can see, solely from being in complete opposition or antithesis to the attitude and movements which, from intelligible causes, are assumed when a dog intends to fight, and which consequently are expressive of anger. I request the reader to look at the four accompanying sketches, which have been given in order to recall vividly the appearance of a dog under these two states of mind. It is, however, not a little difficult to represent affection in a dog, whilst caressing his master and wagging his tail, as the essence of the expression lies in the continuous flexuous movements.

· · · · · · · · · ·

Figure 2.

In these cases of the dog and cat, there is every reason to believe that the gestures both of hostility and affection are innate or inherited; for they are almost identically the same in the different races of the species, and in all the individuals of the same race, both young and old.

I will here give one other instance of antithesis in expression. I formerly possessed a large dog, who, like every other dog, was much pleased to go out walking. He showed his pleasure by trotting gravely before me with high steps, head much raised, moderately erected ears, and tail carried aloft but not stiffly. Not far from my house a path branches off to the right, leading to the hot-house, which I used often to visit for a few moments, to look at my experimental plants. This was always a great disappointment to the dog, as he did not know whether I should continue my walk; and the instantaneous and complete change of expression which came over him as soon as my body swerved in the least towards the path (and I sometimes tried this as an experiment) was laughable. His look of dejection was known to every member of the family, and was called his *hot-house face*. This consisted in the head drooping much, the whole body sinking a little and remaining motionless; the ears and tail falling suddenly down, but the tail was by no means wagged. With the falling of the ears and of his great chaps, the eyes became much changed in appearance, and I fancied that they looked less bright. His aspect was that of piteous, hopeless dejection; and it was, as I have said, laughable, as the cause was so slight. Every detail in his attitude was in complete opposition to his former joyful yet dignified bearing; and can be explained, as it appears to me, in no other way, except through the principle of antithesis. Had not the change been so instantaneous, I should have attributed it to his lowered spirits affecting, as in the case of man, the nervous system and circulation, and consequently the tone of his whole muscular frame; and this may have been in part the cause.

. . . .

Dogs when approaching a strange dog, may find it useful to show by their movements that they are friendly, and do not wish to fight. When two young dogs in play are growling and biting each other's faces and legs, it is obvious that they mutually understand each other's gestures and manners. There seems, indeed, some degree of instinctive knowledge in puppies and kittens, that they must not use their sharp little teeth or claws too freely in their play, though this sometimes happens and a squeal is the result; otherwise they would often injure each other's eyes. When my terrier bites my hand in play, often snarling at the same time, if he bites too hard and I say *gently, gently*, he goes on biting, but answers me by a few wags of the tail, which seems to say "Never mind, it is all fun." Although dogs do thus express, and

12

may wish to express, to other dogs and to man, that they are in a friendly state of mind, it is incredible that they could ever have deliberately thought of drawing back and depressing their ears, instead of holding them erect, — of lowering and wagging their tails, instead of keeping them stiff and upright, &c., because they knew that these movements stood in direct opposition to those assumed under an opposite and savage frame of mind.

Again, when a cat, or rather when some early progenitor of the species, from feeling affectionate first slightly arched its back, held its tail perpendicularly upwards and pricked its ears, can it be believed that the animal consciously wished thus to show that its frame of mind was directly the reverse of that, when from being ready to fight or to spring on its prey, it assumed a crouching attitude, curled its tail from side to side and depressed its ears? Even still less can I believe that my dog voluntarily put on his dejected attitude and "*hot-house face,*" which formed so complete a contrast to his previous cheerful attitude and whole bearing. It cannot be supposed that he knew that I should understand his expression, and that he could thus soften my heart and make me give up visiting the hot-house.

II

I have already described (Figures 1 and 2) the appearance of a dog approaching another dog with hostile intentions, namely, with erected ears, eyes intently directed forwards, hair on the neck and back bristling, gait remarkably stiff, with the tail upright and rigid. So familiar is this appearance to us, that an angry man is sometimes said "to have his back up." Of the above points, the stiff gait and upright tail alone require further discussion . . . .

With respect to the upright position of the tail, it seems to depend (but whether this is really the case I know not) on the elevator muscles being more powerful than the depressors, so that when all the muscles of the hinder part of the body are in a state of tension, the tail is raised. A dog in cheerful spirits, and trotting before his master with high, elastic steps, generally carries his tail aloft, though it is not held nearly so stiffly as when he is angered . . . .

When a dog is on the point of springing on his antagonist, be utters a savage growl; the ears are pressed closely backwards, and the upper lip (Figure 3) is retracted out of the way of his teeth, especially of his canines. These movements may be observed with dogs and puppies in their play. But if a dog gets really savage in his play, his expression immediately changes. This, however, is simply due to the lips and ears being drawn back with much greater energy. If a dog only snarls another, the lip is generally retracted on one side alone, namely towards his enemy.

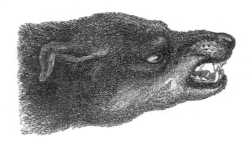

Figure 3.

Figure 4.

The movements of a dog whilst exhibiting affection towards his master were described (Figures 4 and 5). These consist in the head and whole body being lowered and thrown into flexuous movements, with the tail extended and wagged from side to side. The ears fall down and are drawn somewhat backwards, which causes the eyelids to be elongated, and alters the whole appearance of the face. The lips hang loosely, and the hair remains smooth. All these movements or gestures are

14

explicable, as I believe, from their standing in complete antithesis to those naturally assumed by a savage dog under a directly opposite state of mind. When a man merely speaks to, or just notices, his dog, we see the last vestige of these movements in a slight wag of the tail, without any other movement of the body, and without even the ears being lowered. Dogs also exhibit their affection by desiring to rub against their masters, and to be rubbed or patted by them.

. . . .

Figure 5.

Dogs have another and striking way of exhibiting their affection, namely, by licking the hands or faces of their masters. They sometimes lick other dogs, and then it is always their chops. I have also seen dogs licking cats with whom they were friends. This habit probably originated in the females carefully licking their puppies — the dearest object of their love — for the sake of cleansing them. They also often give their puppies, after a short absence, a few cursory licks, apparently from affection. Thus the habit will have become associated with the emotion of love, however it may afterwards be aroused. It is now so firmly inherited or innate, that it is transmitted equally to both sexes. A female terrier of mine lately had her puppies destroyed, and though at all times a very affectionate creature, I was much struck with the manner in which she then tried to satisfy her instinctive maternal love by expending it on me; and her desire to lick my hands rose to an insatiable passion.

The same principle probably explains why dogs, when feeling affectionate, like rubbing against their masters and being rubbed or patted by them, for from the nursing of their puppies, contact with a beloved object has become firmly associated in their minds with the emotion of love.

The feeling of affection of a dog towards his master is combined with a strong sense of submission, which is akin to fear. Hence dogs not only lower their bodies and crouch a little as they approach their masters, but sometimes throw themselves on the ground with their bellies upwards. This is a movement as completely opposite as is possible to any show of resistance. I formerly possessed a large dog who was not at all afraid to fight with other dogs; but a wolf-like shepherd-dog in the neighbourhood, though not ferocious and not so powerful as my dog, had a strange influence over him. When they met on the road, my dog used to run to meet him, with his tail partly tucked in between his legs and hair not erected; and then be would throw himself on the ground, belly upwards. By this action he seemed to say more plainly than by words, "Behold, I am your slave."

A pleasurable and excited state of mind, associated with affection, is exhibited by some dogs in a very peculiar manner, namely, by grinning. This was noticed long ago by Somerville,[3] who says,

> And with a courtly grin, the fawning bound Salutes thee cow'ring, his wide op'ning nose Upward he curls, and his large sloe-back eyes Melt in soft blandishments, and humble joy.   *The Chase*, book i.

---

[3] William Somerville (1675-1742) was a British writer who in 1737 wrote "The Chase," a poem tracing the history of hunting.

16

Sir W. Scott's famous Scotch greyhound, Maida, had this habit, and it is common with terriers.[4] I have also seen it in a Spitz and in a sheep-dog. Mr. Riviere,[5] who has particularly attended to this expression, informs me that it is rarely displayed in a perfect manner, but is quite common in a lesser degree. The upper lip during the act of grinning is retracted, as in snarling, so that the canines are exposed, and the ears are drawn backwards; but the general appearance of the animal clearly shows that anger is not felt. Sir C. Bell[6] remarks "Dogs, in their expression of fondness, have a slight eversion of the lips, and grin and sniff amidst their gambols, in a way that resembles laughter." Some persons speak of the grin as a smile, but if it had been really a smile, we should see a similar, though more pronounced, movement of the lips and ears, when dogs utter their bark of joy; but this is not the case, although a bark of joy often follows a grin. On the other hand, dogs, when playing with their comrades or masters, almost always pretend to bite each other; and they then retract, though not energetically, their lips and ears. Hence I suspect that there is a tendency in some dogs, whenever they feel lively pleasure combined with affection, to act through habit and association on the same muscles, as in playfully biting each other, or their masters' hands.

I have described . . . the gait and appearance of a dog when cheerful, and the marked antithesis presented by the same animal when dejected and disappointed, with his head, ears, body, tail, and chops drooping, and eyes dull. Under the expectation of any great pleasure, dogs bound and jump about in an extravagant manner, and bark for joy. The tendency to bark under this state of mind is inherited, or runs in the breed: greyhounds rarely bark, whilst the Spitz-dog barks so incessantly on starting for a walk with his master that he becomes a nuisance.

An agony of pain is expressed by dogs in nearly the same way as by many other animals, namely, by howling writhing, and contortions of the whole body.

Attention is shown by the head being raised, with the ears erected, and eyes intently directed towards the object or quarter under observation. If it be a sound and the source is not known, the head is often turned obliquely from side to side in a

---

[4] Sir Walter Scott (1771-1802) wrote in *The Talisman* about Scottish deerhounds: "a most perfect creature of heaven . . . of the noblest northern breed . . . deep in the chest, strong in the stern . . . strength to pull down a bull — swiftness to catch an antelope."

[5] Briton Riviere (1840-1920) was a British artist with whom Darwin corresponded concerning canine expressions.

[6] "The Anatomy of Expression as Connected with the Fine Arts," 1844, p. 140. Sir Charles Bell (1774-1842) was a noted Scottish anatomist and Surgeon. His *Essays on the Anatomy of Expression* was first published in 1806.

most significant manner, apparently in order to judge with more exactness from what point the sound proceeds. But I have seen a dog greatly surprised at a new noise, turning, his head to one side through habit, though he clearly perceived the source of the noise. Dogs, as formerly remarked, when their attention is in any way aroused, whilst watching some object, or attending to some sound, often lift up one paw and keep it doubled up, as if to make a slow and stealthy approach.

A dog under extreme terror will throw himself down, howl, and void his excretions; but the hair, I believe, does not become erect unless some anger is felt. I have seen a dog much terrified at a band of musicians who were playing loudly outside the house, with every muscle of his body trembling, with his heart palpitating so quickly that the beats could hardly be counted, and panting for breath with widely open mouth, in the same manner as a terrified man does. Yet this dog had not exerted himself; he had only wandered slowly and restlessly about the room, and the day was cold.

Even a very slight degree of fear is invariably shown by the tail being tucked in between the legs. This tucking in of the tail is accompanied by the ears being drawn backwards; but they are not pressed closely to the head, as in snarling, and they are not lowered, as when a dog is pleased or affectionate. When two young dogs chase each other in play, the one that runs away always keeps his tail tucked inwards. So it is when a dog, in the highest spirits, careens like a mad creature round and round his master in circles, or in figures of eight. He then acts as if another dog were chasing him. This curious kind of play, which must be familiar to every one who has attended to dogs, is particularly apt to be excited, after the animal has been a little startled or frightened, as by his master suddenly jumping out on him in the dusk. In this case, as well as when two young dogs are chasing each other in play, it appears as if the one that runs away was afraid of the other catching him by the tail; but as far as I can find out, dogs very rarely catch each other in this manner. I asked a gentleman, who had kept foxhounds all his life, and he applied to other experienced sportsmen, whether they had ever seen hounds thus seize a fox; but they never had. It appears that when a dog is chased, or when in danger of being struck behind, or of anything falling on him, in all these cases he wishes to withdraw as quickly as possible his whole hind-quarters, and that from some sympathy or connection between the muscles, the tail is then drawn closely inwards.

. . . .

As I have said, when a dog is chased and runs away, he keeps his ears directed backwards but still open; and this is clearly done for the sake of hearing the footsteps of his pursuer. From habit the ears are often held in this same position, and

18

the tail tucked in, when the danger is obviously in front. I have repeatedly noticed, with a timid terrier of mine, that when she is afraid of some object in front, the nature of which she perfectly knows and does not need to reconnoiter, yet she will for a long time hold her ears and tail in this position, looking the image of discomfort. Discomfort, without any fear, is similarly expressed: thus, one day I went out of doors, just at the time when this same dog knew that her dinner would be brought. I did not call her, but she wished much to accompany me, and at the same time she wished much for her dinner; and there she stood, first looking one way and then the other, with her tail tucked in and ears drawn back, presenting an unmistakable appearance of perplexed discomfort.

Almost all the expressive movements now described, with the exception of the grinning from joy, are innate or instinctive, for they are common to all the individuals, young and old, of all the breeds. Most of them are likewise common to the aboriginal parents of the dog, namely the wolf and jackal; and some of them to other species of the same group.

. . . .

Sufficient facts have now been given with respect to the expressions of various animals. . . . . He who will look at a dog preparing to attack another dog or a man, and at the same animal when caressing his master, or will watch the countenance of a monkey when insulted, and when fondled by his keeper, will be forced to admit that the movements of their features and their gestures are almost as expressive as those of man.

———————

4

The Consciousness of Dogs [1]
(1872)

Frances Power Cobbe

Frances Power Cobbe (1822-1904) was a sociologically astute Anglo-Irish theorist, writer, suffragist and anti-vivisectionist. Born in Dublin, she eventually moved to England.[2] Today, Cobbe is an acknowledged early social theorist.[3] She presented an especially important paper to the Social Science Congress in 1862 on permitting women to sit for university examinations. Her major books include: *Essays on the Pursuits of Women* (1863), *Darwinism in Morals* (1872); *False Beasts and True: Essays on Natural and Unnatural History* (1875); *The Life of Frances Power Cobbe* (1895); *The Duties of Women: A Course of Lectures* (1898). She heard Harriet Martineau's brother, James, preach and lecture over the course of several years and once tried to meet Harriet Martineau, but received the response, "I need not say how happy I should have been to become  acquainted with Miss Cobbe; but the time is past and I am only fit for old friends who can excuse my shortcomings. I have lost ground so much of late that the case is clear. I must give up all hopes of so great a pleasure."[4] Cobbe's intellectual circle included Charles Darwin,

---

[1] Edited from the *Quarterly Review* 133 (October 1872: 419-51). Various examples, anecdotes, and archaic references have been omitted to conserve space. See also: Frances Power Cobbe, "Dogs Whom I have Met," *Cornhill Magazine* 26 (December 1872: 662-78).

[2] For greater biographical detail, see: Cobbe's autobiography, *The Life of Frances Power Cobbe* (especially Vol. II, pp. 556-634 on "The Claims of Brutes") and S. Mitchell, *Frances Power Cobbe: Victorian Feminist, Journalist, Reformer* (University of Virginia Press, 2004).

[3] L. McDonald, *Women Theorists on Society and Politics* (Wilfred Laurier University Press, 1998: 248-58).

[4] F.P. Cobbe, *The Life of Frances Power Cobbe*, vol. 2 (Houghton, Mifflin, 1895: 522).

among others.[5] Cobbe's archival papers can be found in several repositories, including the Huntington Library (San Marino, California), the Women's Suffrage Collection (Manchester Central Library, Manchester, England), and Vassar College Archives (Poughkeepsie, New York). The records of the British Union for the Abolition of Vivisection, founded by Cobbe in 1898, are housed at the University of Hull (Hull, England).

SCORES OF BOOKS, of which [those noted below] are samples,[6] offer us materials for estimating the capabilities and characteristics of dogs. With such wealth of experience, and aided by the sympathetic attention which many of us personally give to our favourites, it ought not to be impossible to construct something like an outline of Canine Psychology. We ought to be able to work out the problem, "How a Dog Thinks and Feels," if not with certainty, yet with what must approve itself as a near approach to truth. In the case of an Intelligence above our own, the attempt to realize its consciousness and conditions of being by any effort of thought — *wherever it surpasses us* — must obviously be futile, or, at best, can only supply us with such a "representative truth" as the idea which a man born blind may obtain of the nature of colour. But the indolent assumption that the same inability attends us in the case of the lower animals, whose natures our own seem to comprise and overlap on all sides, is far from justified by any inherent difficulty in the matter. Extreme patience in working out details; caution in refraining from leaping to the conclusion that the possession of any single manlike faculty implies that of another; and above all, the "scientific use of the Imagination," warmed by sympathy with "Our Poor Relations," appear sufficient to supply the full equipment of our task. Proceeding step by step, and carefully distinguishing everything

---

[5] See: Darwin's letter to Cobbe, reproduced below as Chapter 5, this volume.

[6] George R. Jesse, *Researches into the History of the British Dog* (London, 1866); E.B. Hamley, *Our Poor Relations* (Edinburgh and London, 1872); John Selbey Watson, *The Reasoning Power in Animals* (London, 1867); Edward Jesse, *Anecdotes of Dogs* (London, 1858); Charles Hamilton Smith, *The Dog* (London, 1865); Delabere Blaine, *Canine Pathology* (London, 1841); W.N. Hutchinson, *Dog Breaking* (London, 1856); W.C.L. Martin, *The History of the Dog* (London, 1845); Stonehenge, *The Days of the British Islands* (London, 1872); Edward Mayhew, *Dogs and their Management* (London, 1869); Society for the Prevention of Cruelty, *The Animal World: A Monthly Advocate of Humanity*, Vol. III; Idstone, *The Dog* (London, 1872).

noteworthy which dogs have been observed to do, for that which experience proves to be beyond their powers, we may map out a line which shall approximately represent the circumference of their natures. Within this circle — as Thought is still Thought, in whatsoever brain it be carried on, and Love is Love in every breast which beats with its emotion, — we are justified in assuming that there is a real correspondence and similarity between the mental processes and feelings of the animal and our own. When we endeavour in such manner to realize the consciousness of a dog by fancying ourselves circumscribed by his limitations, we are using no idle play of imagination, but pursing our inquiry by a method almost as exact as that, so favoured by modern mathematicians, of applying one figure to another. How far the special attributes which distinguish us from all the lower animals, must modify each detail of thought and feeling; how Self-Consciousness must bring a new factor into every thought, and Moral Free Agency a new element into every passion, it should be part of our work to endeavour to trace. But, as above remarked, though it would be impossible for the lower being to add by imagination any such gifts to his consciousness, it is by no means an impossible task, albeit a delicate one, for the higher to imagine himself divested of them. The combination of the unconsciousness of infancy with the eager feelings and irresponsibility of childhood would not indeed accurately represent the state required, for, after the stage of strange physical similarity before birth between man and the dog, discovered by Professor Haeckel,[7] there is no epoch in the life of the human child when a perfect parallel between it and the animal, either as regards body or mind, can be justly instituted. But picking out the points in our own experience which we share with the brute, and cautiously eliminating those which the brute does not share with us, we must needs be on the right track for constructing — as the well-worn joke would describe it — his consciousness out of our own. Our business, then, is neither like the old fabulists and modern writers of children's story-books, to talk of dogs as if they were men who had undergone metempsychosis and brought human thought and feeling into canine forms; nor yet to rest solemnly satisfied, like the old Egyptians, to treat our familiar companions as if they were so many four-footed Mysteries altogether beyond our comprehension. Modern Science is bound to show, both what the beast is in his *for intérieur*, and where and how he at present falls short of a man; — even if Mr. Darwin may hold out hopes that a million years to come the dog's

---

[7] Ernst Haeckel (1834-1919) was a German zoologist who became a strong advocate of Darwinism.

posterity may develop into a race of saints and sages, of a loftier type than those whom we have known descended from the far less amiable and heroic Simian stock![8]

Before attempting to delineate the first outlines of a Dog's Consciousness, it will be desirable to recapitulate as briefly as possible the principal circumstances which determine his physical condition relatively to our own, and thence work upward to the study of his emotional and mental characteristics. The dog, as compared to man, has against him: —

1st. Inferiority of size, keeping him always beside his master like a dwarf with a giant. The legs of men, rather than their faces, must form the prominent objects of his view; and the agreeable sense of looking down with condescension on something smaller than ourselves, so obviously enjoyed by a big dog over a little one, must be reversed into a deep sense of humiliation as regards the lordly race who tower over him.

2nd. The lack of hands, which forbids to the cleverest dog the use of the most rudimentary mechanical contrivance, even such as crushing a bone with a stone. A dog trying to roll himself in a blanket, or to leap up a tree, reveals the vast difference between his instruments and those of a cat whose claws will aid her to climb; or of a bird, whose beak answers the purpose of a single finger and opposable thumb.

3rd. The dog's vocal organs, though seemingly more like ours than the hard black tongues and beaks of parrots, are yet incapable of being used for the formation of sounds more articulate than belong to speechless human beings. He is emphatically what the Irish expressively call him, a "poor dumb beast," though he is able to understand human language to an extent which only those who carefully watch him can credit.

4th. Of the inferiority of the dog's brain to that of a man it is needless to speak, seeing that it is the point which doubtless determines most of the other conditions of the animal's being. A quadruped of the size of a dog, possessed of a brain of human dimensions, would, even if dumb, be assuredly something very different from a dog.

5th. Lastly, among the great disadvantages of the dog, one which most effectually bars his advance, is the shortness of his term of life. The oldest dog only attains the age when a boy begins to acquire his higher powers; and dies before reason and conscience, or even the stronger affections, are fairly developed in his human contemporary. We blame our "stupid old dog" at ten years of age, when we should excuse our son's folly, with the observation, "Poor little child!" What

---

[8] For Cobbe's critical position regarding Charles Darwin, see: *Darwin in Morals, and other Essays* (London: Williams and Norgate, 1872).

wisdom a dog would attain who should live to the length of span, and could celebrate a "Golden" anniversary of devotion to his master, it is almost painful to think. The creature would have arrived at a point of intelligence whereat his physical defects would press on him as on a dumb or maimed human being; and, for ourselves, the pain of separation would be intolerable. The death of the fond companion of a dozen years is quite sad enough; that of a dog who had followed our steps from the cradle to old age would trespass too closely on the sacred borders of human bereavement.

These various physical disadvantages result, in the case of the dog, as in that of all the lower animals, in the supreme deficiency which cuts off the entail of progress at each generation. The brute has no tradition, oral or written, and, though he inherits propensities from his progenitors, and copies his parents when brought up with them, he receives so little direct guidance from them, that he is not perceptibly less intelligent when kept entirely apart from his own kind in such isolation as makes of a human child almost an idiot. Like our own, the "set" of the dog's brain is determined by the habits of preceding generations, and the facility for receiving education is inherited from an educated ancestry. But the positive information which a human being receives from the hour he begins to understand language to the last moment of life, from nurse, mother, companions, teachers, preachers and books, is utterly denied to the dog, who must acquire every item of his knowledge directly through his own sense. When we think of all that this implies, and what infinitesimally small store of facts or reflections the most intelligent man could acquire on such terms in seventy years, the wonder becomes rather how much, than how little, is known by a dog who has but ten or twelve years in which to learn everything.

Against all these disadvantages — diminutive size, lack of hands, lack of language, small brain, short life, total want of traditional experience — a dog, so far as we can see, can only set one single special physical advantage which he possesses over us. With us the sense of smelling is but slightly developed, and though it is an inlet of pleasurable or disagreeable emotions, and possesses a singular power of awakening associations of memory, it is of extremely little use to us as an organ of mental information. Even when we do obtain an idea by way of the nose, we commonly treat it with distrust as more uncertain than one derived from eyesight or hearing, and hesitate to swear in a court of justice that we have positively smelled even such highly odorous things as brandy or gunpowder. But in the case of our canine friend all this is altered. He learns from smell quite as much as from his sight or his hearing; and it is clear that he is even more disposed to rely on this sense than on any other. All day long that curious little black organ at the tip of his nose is inquiring actively whatever it can sniff out about people and things; and when his owner returns after an absence, though the dog partially recognizes his aspect and

24

voice at a distance, he never gives himself up to rapture til he has smelt him, and so placed his identity beyond the hazards of a Tichborne suit.[9]

But the dog's sense of smell differs from our own not only in superior acuteness, but also in another way which is not equally a subject of congratulation. The pleasures and pains he derives from odours seem to be nearly exactly the reverse of our own, and he loves what we hate, and hates what we love . . . . As no prospect yet appears of converting dogs to our views in these matters, it is to be feared that the love of objectionable odours must long cause a breach in the continuity of sympathy between us and our humble companions . . . .

Whether we ought to consider the marvellous faculty possessed by dogs, cats, and many other animals, of finding their way for long distances by unknown roads, as an exhibition of their immense acuteness of olfactory perception, or rather as evidence of the possession of a specific sense different from any which we have yet recognized, is a question of great interest to which it would be impossible here to do justice. In all collections of anecdotes of dogs instances of the display of this faculty are put forward as evidences of the sagacity of the animal; but it is certain that no sagacity, in the ordinary meaning of the term, without the aid of a sense different from any known to us, would enable the creature to perform some of the feats so recorded . . . .

It does not appear that this singular faculty is peculiar to dogs, or a mark of their superior intelligence. Cats, ducks, and many other creatures have made similar journeys; and, in truth, the annual migrations of so many tribes of birds and fishes can hardly be explained but as exhibitions of the same power. The only situation in which animals seem to lose themselves is in the streets of a great city, and where the very cleverest of dogs, even notably retrievers (as the keepers of the admirable Home for Lost Dogs will testify), fail to find their way for very short distances . . . .

To realize, then, the physical conditions of a dog, we must imagine ourselves inhabiting a diminutive and prostrate form, without hands, without speech, and destined to die of old age as we enter our teens; also, as having for our special endowments a remarkable power of finding our way, and a preternaturally acute nose, accompanied by an unconquerable propensity for Ubomi, and all Ubominable things. It may be added that we should conceive our bodies covered with hair; and that, beside the possession of great swiftness and agility, we are gifted with a peculiar caudal appendage, serving, so effectually, as a "vehicle for the emotions,"

---

[9] The Tichborn trials, conducted from 1871 to 1873, eventually found that Arthur Orton was an imposter who falsely claimed to be Sir Roger Tichborn, the rightful (but by then deceased) heir to a family estate.

that instead of availing, like language, "to conceal our thoughts," it should constantly and involuntarily betray our joy, sorrow, alarm, or rage.

Some of the immediate consequences of these physical conditions of the dog should be noted before we go further. In the first place, his inability to speak forces him to devise ingenious ways of making his wants understood; such as the artifice of a dog belonging to the writer, who, finding her bowl of water frozen in a frost, established herself in a corner where another bowl had been kept two years previously, and sat there looking mournfully at her owner till her sad case was perceived. When a brute lives with people too busy or too obtuse to attend to such signals, he becomes sad and depressed, and loses all originality . . . . The pantomime of dogs, their scratching at doors for admittance, their beseeching entreaties to be taken out walking, their ardent invitations to visit their puppies, are all somewhat affecting instances of the painful efforts of the creatures to express what we should say in two words.

Again, another consequence of the dog's lack of language, which curiously differentiates his life from ours, is that he can be told nothing beforehand, so that all his sorrows remain uncheered by hope, and all his pleasures have the keen charm of the *imprévu*. Few things are more pitiable than to see an animal after his master's departure going about miserably seeking him, unable to receive the consolation of the assurance that the being in whom his whole heart is centered will by-and-by return. After one such period of anxiety, terminated by the joy of restoration, he does not give way to equal despair, being supported by hope born of experience, but he knows perfectly well evermore how to interpret the signs of an approaching journey, and scores of times has been known to hide himself in his master's trunk, hoping to be carried with him. On the other hand, a dog's delights are never chilled or forestalled by expectation . . . .

Passing beyond the physical conditions of the dog and their immediate results, we now proceed a step further towards constructing an idea of his Consciousness, by studying his Emotions, and comparing them with our own. A little reflection shows that a dog approaches a man much more nearly in the matter of feeling than either of physical or mental characteristics. It is a startling fact, well brought out by Jesse in a synopsis of the dog's attributes (*Researches*, chap. v.), that there are very few human passions which a dog does not share . . . .

[T]he following long list of passions and emotions [are shared by the dog with ourselves]: anger, hatred, jealousy, envy, gluttony, love, fear, pride, vanity, magnanimity, chivalry, covetousness, avarice, shame, humour, gratitude, regret, grief, maternal love, courage, fortitude, hope, and faith. The line delineating the circumference of the dog's nature must include all these; and many of them in a highly developed form. We must leave outside, as passions of which the dog does

26

not partake, 1st, the love of intoxicants[10] (a passion having only its peculiar significance in a moral free agent); 2nd, modesty (also pertaining exclusively to beings possessed of self-control); and, 3rdly and finally, the whole lofty range of feelings which have abstract ideas for their objects, to which his intellectual status forbids him to ascend. The dog obviously cannot love art, science, or literature, simply because his mental faculties fall short of apprehending the topics concerned. That he has any aesthetic sense, any notion of the beautiful or of the sublime in nature is more than doubtful; and his insatiable curiosity which, if allied to higher powers would form the spring of scientific research, ends, in his case, with the accumulation of practically useful facts. Thus we arrive at the conclusion that the line which shall delineate the circumference of the dog's emotional nature must *exclude* all those passions of humanity which are directed to abstract objects, and *include* nearly the entire range of those which concern the gratification of the physical desires and personal affections.

To these cardinal passions, shared by all men and dogs, should next be added certain special propensities partaken by certain dogs with certain men. Foremost of these is the passion for the Chase – a sentiment which the gentlemen of England, at all events, cannot find it difficult to imagine as pertaining to their own consciousness. To describe the share it holds in the life of the majority of dogs, and the degree to which their intelligence unfolds in the congenial pursuit, would swell this paper to a volume. Another propensity which the dog partially shares with men is the Histrionic. Nobody who has watched a dog closely can doubt that he frequently amuses himself by performing an imaginary scene and representing an unreal passion. At one moment he acts a dog in a rage, and pretends to be savage, and the next he acts a dog in terror, and runs round barking wildly . . . . Playing with a puppy half his size he pretends to fly with tail down and ears laid back, scampering as if for his life. With his comparison dog or cat he constantly performs an impromptu drama of the sensational kind, whose "*motif*" is generally an imaginary quarrel. After a fearful amount of struggling, biting, and growling, in which excellent care is taken that neither of the performers receive the smallest hurt, he finally pretends to throttle his victim, and enacts the closing scene with a tragic *furore* . . . .

There remain now to be considered only certain higher feelings – the sympathetic, the religious, and the moral — whose possession by dogs are all commonly denied. It has been asserted, over and over again, that one of the chief

---

[10] With due respect to Cobbe, the editors have encountered a few beer-drinking dogs — albeit said consumption was sadly aided and abetted by humans who procured the alcohol. See: D.M. Houston and L.L. Head, "Acute Alcohol Intoxication in a Dog," *Canadian Veterinary Journal*, 34 (January, 1993: 41-42).

distinctions between man and the races below him lies in his Sympathy; that brutes kill or forsake their disabled companions, and man alone pities and assists his brother . . . .

It is clear at first sight that animals have, as a rule, far less power of sympathy than civilized man, and that there exists in many of their tribes an instinct of a contrary sort (very painful to witness, though undoubtedly beneficent in its general action) to destroy the wounded and decrepit. Nevertheless it appears to be entirely an error to suppose that the higher animals are without that sense of pain at the sight of pain of others wherein consists the first element of human sympathy . . . . [Numerous anecdotes] prove the most difficult part of our problem, namely, the capacity of dogs to sympathize with their own kind. As to their power of sympathizing with man, it is a matter concerning which no one possessed of an attached dog ever entertained a doubt. The dejection of the dog when his master is in affliction, his feverish anxiety when he is ill, his fury when he is struck by a foe or operated on by a surgeon, his fond efforts at consolation at sight of his tears, and his demonstrations of ecstacy at his restoration to health and cheerfulness, are all fact equally familiar and affecting. How many lonely, deceived, and embittered hearts have been saved from breaking or turning to stone by the humble sympathy of a dog, He who saw them alone can tell . . . .

[I]n endeavouring to construct an idea of the Consciousness of a dog, we seem bound to include in it a sentiment corresponding singularly with that which in ourselves we name the Religious, but which differs from ours by two sad distinctions. First, the dog worships a being always imperfect, and often cruel; and secondly, he worships him with a blind homage which never ascends to that rational moral allegiance of a free human soul . . . .

Superstition, or the awe of the Unknown, has been treated by some thinkers as the primary germ of religion, and by others, far more justly, as its shadow. This shadow certainly falls on the dog no less than on man. The bravest dog will continually show signs of terror at the sight of an object he does not understand, such as the skin of a dead monkey, the snake of a hookah, a pair of bellows or a rattle. That the animal fancies there is something more than merely dangerous, something "uncanny" and preternatural about such things, is apparent from his behaviour, which in the case of real danger is aggressively daring, and in that of imaginary peril abjectly timorous . . . .

The Moral nature of dogs, which must now be discussed, offers the most difficult of the problems concerning them . . . . [W]e must carefully keep in mind the often forgotten distinction between the possession of the most generous and beautiful impulses, and the power to exert a choice between following them, or others of a lower nature. That the dog possesses the noblest impulses is beyond a doubt . . . . But

28

a dog has many low impulses, as well as many high ones; and before we properly recognize him as a moral agent, it would be needful to show that he can exercise discrimination between the two.

That a dog has a Will and choice of action in the vulgar sense, it would be idle to deny. Nothing, indeed, is more *wilful* than the animal thus understood, insomuch that "bulldog tenacity" has become a proverb. Obviously, too, he is often "of two minds," whether he will follow one person or another, obey his master or enjoy an escapade; and the final decision is made on the balance of his likings and dislikings, fears and hopes. Does this Wilfulness then constitute the dog a Moral Free Agent, and must responsibility accompany such exercise of volition? Certainly not. But to find ground on which to deny his responsibility while admitting his wilfulness, we must go far below the superficial idea of moral freedom commonly in vogue, and fall back on some such theory as that of Kant . . . . That the dog has any Moral Freedom of the real sort is more than doubtful . . . .

We have seen how a dog Feels, we must endeavour to form an idea how he Thinks. Recurring to our postulate that Thought is Thought in whatsoever brain it be carried on, and dismissing the vain attempt to distinguish between Instinct and Reason as probably arbitrary and certainly beside the purpose of our investigation, we may proceed to trace, so far as our materials permit, the circumference of the dog's mental powers. The following facts may severe as points to guide our outline. In the first place the mechanism of a dog's mind obviously includes several of the same wheels and pulleys as our own. He has *Memory* of persons, places, and events, extending backward to his early youth, and it is stirred, precisely like ours, according to the same law of *association of ideas*. When his master has deserted him, and in his despair the dog takes some cast-off garment and lies upon it for days together, growling at every one who tries to lure him away, what can we suppose he is doing? Obviously he is using the old coat or shoe, to bring him nearer to his lost friend; just as many of us have treasured a flower or a lock of hair; or as a hagiolater kneels beside the relics of his saint. Further, association of ideas enables him often in default of language to understand what men are doing about him. Having once seen guns elaborately cleaned preparatory to the 12th of August,[11] the sight of the process next year fills him with rapturous anticipation of sport. The little differences of Sunday hours and costumes prove to him the hopelessness of an invitation to the walk which is to end at church. On other days the taking up of a hat, or stick, is enough to make him leap for joy, the exhibition of a whip to cringe, and the sight of

---

[11] As codified by the Game Act of 1831, August 12 was the traditional start of the hunting season for grouse and ptarmigan in the U.K. Harriet Martineau explored the wider social implications of this legislation in her *Forest and Game-Law Tales* (Edward Moxon, 1845-1846).

a trunk, to enter into paroxysms of anxiety. Beside memory and association of ideas — both working in his narrow sphere, probably, as perfectly as they act in our wider one — the dog may be proved to possess a certain share of *Fancy* or *Imagination*. The remarks made regarding his propensity to act little dramas, showed thus much, at all events, as also his habit of fancying something terrible in odd-looking objects. By his dreams it is manifest that he either exactly reproduces by involuntary cerebration the precise events impressed on his memory, or, as is much more probable, that his brain, like ours, weaves them into fresh combinations. In the latter case, and supposing the dog to have a real dream of an imaginary chase after a hare, or battle with a cat, it almost necessarily follows that he can exercise the same faculty of pure Imagination awake, and that when he likes blinking in the sun or on the rug, he follows out, in his own little way, a reverie, much like our own, combining what has been and what might be, in a visionary scene of which either hope or fear acts as the scene-shifter. *Judgment*, or an intelligent decision between probabilities, is unquestionably one of the faculties of a dog. A clever dog is one of the best discriminators of character in the world. He distinguishes at a glace a tramp or swell-mobsman from a gentleman even in the most soiled attire. He has also a keen sense of the relative importance of persons, and never fails to know who is the master of the house. By the help of these faculties, memory, association of ideas, fancy, and judgment, a dog can make plans and deliberately arrange how to compass his ends . . . .

From such a general view of canine intelligence, it appears an irresistible conclusion that all (or nearly all) the elementary machinery of the human mind is present and active in the brain of a dog. There are Memory, Reflection, Combination, Forethought, Association of Ideas, and that process of arguing from cause to effect which we are wont to consider as Reasoning, strictly so called. The limitations within which this mental machinery works are indeed narrow, seldom proceeding beyond three or four steps at furthest, and dealing only, so far as we can guess, with matters immediately perceived by the senses; but nevertheless it is incumbent on us to recognize that, *so far as it goes*, the thought of a dog is the same sort of phenomenon as the thought of a man, carried on doubtless with similar modifications of cerebral matter, and being to the creature who thinks, to all intents and purposes the same action.

To comprehend what it would be to think under the conditions which limit the thoughts of a dog, we have need in the first place, to endeavour clearly to realize what it would be to think without Language — not merely as a dumb individual in a speaking race, but as a dumb creature in a dumb race, not even possessed of hands wherewith to make an alphabet of signs. Under such conditions it is apparent that we should hold a wholly different intellectual rank from that which we possess as master of this matchless instrument. It is not only for communication with our fellows but for all the higher processes of thought that words are indispensable, and without their use the finest human brain would be able to conduct its operations a very little way in comparison of the long ascents it performs with the aid of such a ladder. All thought which rises above mere reverie, is a more or less defined *thinking in words*; and the more serious and weighty are our lucubrations, and the more abstruse their theme, the more we need definite language to carry them on. When a man loses the free use of his native tongue in acquiring familiarity with another, he frequently observes the important influence on his thought exercised by the transition when he begins to think in the new language; and every one who has attempted to grapple with questions of metaphysics and ontology is well aware how indispensable to such labour are the tool provided by a philosophical vocabulary. Geometry [for example] could not proceed beyond the simplest propositions without an accurate terminology . . . .

Lastly, we reach the concluding problem of the dog's Consciousness. Human thought is not only occupied with its *objects*, but also carries with it more or less self-consciousness of its *subject*. It turns outward to the world, and also inward. Endless profound things have been written about this self-conscious "Ich," which we carry with us in every soaring and diving of imagination and reason — this "Ego," whose antagonism to the "non-ego" is said to be the first perception of the awakening mind. But, whatever be its mysterious significance, are we bound to limit it to the mind of a man, and to hold that the dog's mind never turns inwards — that he never thinks that marvellous thought "*I am*"?

It has been long ago assumed that so it is; that the animal never gathers up memory and consciousness into one personality; never studies himself or compares himself with other beings, or thinks "I am a dog." Such self-consciousness, the sense of moral responsibility, and the power of forming abstract ideas, are, in truth, it would appear, three phases of the same thing — three things which must exist together or not at all. If the evidence that dogs have no moral responsibility and no abstract ideas be sufficient, the further fact of their having no self-consciousness may be taken for granted; even if the absolute simplicity of their demeanour did not bear with it an assurance, beyond need of argument, that none of the doublings of self-introspection have ever disturbed the pellucid simplicity of their emotions and thoughts.

How, then, does a dog actually think, if he never carries his self-consciousness along with him? Let us remember the hours when that "Old Man of the Sea" has sat lightest on our own shoulders; when, acting at the bidding of some strong feeling, or engrossed in some deep interest, we forgot almost entirely to reflect in our usual wearisome way that "I" am doing this, that, or the other. Let us study the mental condition of the more light-hearted race of men, of children, and of [non-modern peoples]. By a little further development of such experiences we shall find ourselves not far off from the point of the dog's state of mind. Merely to suppose ourselves always engrossed in what we are doing, as we are, for example, when we are reading or writing eagerly, watching a man in danger, or entering some sublime scene — and the feat is achieved. As we feel then, so the dog, in his own little sphere of interests, must feel always.

To sum up the conclusions arrived at in this paper. The dog's physical nature is, in every respect save his keener sense of smelling, inferior to our own. In the region of the passions and emotions he approaches us most nearly, falling short of us only where his intellect fails to append the abstract objects which engage our feelings. Of moral free agency he does not partake; but his allegiance to man supplies him with a shadow of Duty and a Religion *minus* the moral element. Lastly, his mental faculties include all the fundamental machinery of the human intellect, and stop short only where the lack of language bars the path of consecutive reasoning, and in the absence of self-consciousness makes self-introspection impossible.

If these views be correct, it would appear that a dog's consciousness lies in a circle wholly within the borders of our own . . . . He lies indeed far beneath us in the scale of existence; but it is not at a distance wholly *incommensurate*. There is a proportion, albeit a remote one, between him and ourselves . . . .

5

A Letter to Frances Power Cobbe
Concerning "The Consciousness of Dogs" [1]
(1872)

Charles Darwin

November 28th, 1872

[Dear Miss Cobbe,]

I have been greatly interested by your article in the "Quarterly."[2] It seems to me the best analysis of the mind of an animal which I have ever read, and I agree with you on most points. I have been particularly glad to read what you say about the reasoning power of dogs, and about that rather vague matter, their self-consciousness. I dare say however that you would prefer criticism to admiration.

I regret you quote J. so often.[3] I made inquires about one case (which quite broke down) from a man who certainly ought to know Mr. J. well; and I was cautioned that he had not written in a scientific spirit. I regret also that you quote old writers. It may be very illiberal, but their statements go for nothing with me and I suspect with many others. It passes my powers of belief that dogs ever commit suicide. Assuming the statements to be true, I should think it more probable that they were distraught, and did not know what they were doing; nor am I able to credit about fetishes.

One of the most interesting subjects in your article seems to me to be about the moral sense. Since publishing the "Descent of Man" I have got to believe rather more than I did in dogs having what may be called a conscience. When an honorable dog has committed an undiscovered offence he certainly seems *ashamed* (and this is the term naturally and often used) rather than *afraid* to meet his master. My dog, the beloved and beautiful Polly, is at such times extremely affectionate towards me;

---

[1] Edited from Frances Power Cobbe, *Life of Frances Power Cobbe* (Boston: Houghton, Mifflin, 1895, vol. II, pp. 447-48).

[2] "The Consciousness of Dogs," *Quarterly Review* 133 (October 1872: 419-51). For an abridged version, see: Chapter 4, this volume.

[3] Darwin's reference here is possibly to Edward Jesse, author of *Anecdotes of Dogs* (1858) or George R. Jesse, author of *Researches into the History of the British Dog* (1866).

and this leads me to mention a little anecdote. When I was a very little boy, I had committed some offence, so that my conscience troubled me, and when I met my father, I lavished so much affection on him, that he at once asked me what I had done, and told me to confess. I was so utterly confounded at his suspecting anything, that I remember the scene clearly to the present day, and it seems to me that Polly's frame of mind on such occasions is much the same as was mine, for I was not then at all afraid of my father.

[/Signed/ — Charles Darwin]

———————————

6

Variety in Dogs and their Masters [1]
(1872)

Frances Powers Cobbe

THERE ARE FEW THINGS more irritating to one who consistently honors dogs than to hear superficial and indiscriminate people talk of those animals as if they were all alike in their mental and moral qualities, and only differed from each other by being white or black, rough-haired or silky-coated. "*The* dog," these persons will complacently observe, "is" this, that, or the other — "sagacious," "intelligent," and "Fond of the chase." Or they will confide to you that "they like dogs in their proper place " (to wit, somewhere wholly out of sight), or "do not particularly care for a dog." They might just as well remark that "*the* man is wise, honest, and plays the fiddle;" or that " they like human beings when they keep their distance;" or "do not specially care for a man!" That every dog has his idiosyncrasy no less than his master has his own; that his capacities, tempers, gifts, graces, and propensities, vary through the whole gamut of intellect, will, and emotion; and that it would be quite as easy to find two human as two canine Sosias[2] are facts which the vulgar and dog-ignorant mind has never grasped. He who has once loved a dog, if he find courage after its loss to seek a second friend, nearly always endeavors to procure one of the same breed, and, if possible, of the same family, for his heart is drawn to such an animal by its likeness to the dead.; nor can he by any means transfer his affections from the bold and brave mastiff to the tender little King Charles, nor from the fawn-like, coquettish Pomeranian to the sturdy and- matter-of-fact Scotch terrier. But when the nearest approach possible to the lost favorite has been found and installed in his place, the second dog's individuality is never for a moment obliterated, but, on the contrary, comes out every day in more vivid contrast to that of his predecessor. The old pet was perhaps somewhat narrow-minded — a dog of one idea, and that idea was his master. To the rest of mankind he was

---

[1] Edited from Cobbe's "Dogs Whom I Have Met," *Cornhill Magazine* 26 (December 1872: 662-78).

[2] Sosia, a living double; derived from a character of the same name in *Amphitryon*, a comedy of errors by the Roman playwright Maccius Plautus (circa 254-184 BC).

reserved, if not indifferent; and, if forsaken for a time, he pined and refused to be comforted. His successor probably possesses the "Enthusiasm of Humanity" to a degree which often involves him in trouble in consequence of untimely caresses offered with muddy paws to unappreciative strangers, but which reassures us regarding his power to receive consolation in case of our premature departure for a world into which we make no efforts, like the mighty hunters of old, to compel our dogs to follow us. Again, our first dog, after a reprimand, used to shrink from us for hours, and. convey by sad and solemn looks his sense that a cruel breach. had been made in the harmony of our relations. The second will hasten to assure us that we are most graciously forgiven for our bad temper, and that, with all our faults, he loves us still. Number One was addicted to the pleasures of (or under) the table, and displayed his feelings towards bones with unaffected simplicity. Number Two will blink at us urbanely as we proceed with our meal, and only towards the close of the entertainment, when the dreadful idea occurs to him that the courses are over, the dinner is ended, and he is not fed, will he rise in remonstrance on his hind legs and sit like a statue of Anubis[3] till his wants be supplied. Number One was a dog of resources; and when his path of life was beset with any of the thorns which, alas! strew the road which dogs are born to tread — if a door were shut through which he desired to pass, or his water-basin were left unfilled when he was thirsty, or the rat he hoped to catch had retired into an inaccessible hole, — he would employ his whole energy and ingenuity by scratching, whining, begging, watching and poking all round. the premises till he had attained his end. Number Two, on the other hand, when defeated in his first eager rush, always subsides rapidly and resignedly into quiescence, and seeks ere long that peculiar consolation for unsatisfied longings which is to be found in rolling oneself up into the nearest approach to a circle attainable to the vertebrata.

Our first dog seemed to live in an atmosphere of "refined and gentle melancholy," such as the divines of the last generation considered the proper tone of feeling for mortals traveling through this Vale of Tears.[4] His great mournful eyes looked as if they might at any time overflow with drops from the depths of a divine despair, and only when he laid his noble head sadly on the tablecloth, and unmistakably turned those eloquent orbs in unutterable longing towards the dish of biscuits, were we able to fathom the profundity of his sorrow and his aspirations. Our

---

[3] Anubis, an ancient Egyptian god — part human, part jackal — was sometimes depicted sitting loyally atop burial tombs that he protected.

[4] The "vale of tears," in Christian literature, refers to the distress, sorrows and trials of earthly life. See: Psalm 84, verse 6.

36

second dog, on the contrary, is blessed with a cheerful disposition, and evidently views the world as a place abounding in kind people, social dogs, interesting rabbits, and abundant bones. His bark is like the laugh of childhood, and means nothing but that best of all possible jokes, "How happy I am!" He skips here and there as if wishing to go every way at once, and pursues the swallows and leaps at the butterflies out of mere joyousness of heart. And yet, again, Number One had an Oriental indifference for all proceedings not immediately concerning himself, and habitually lay down to enjoy his "kef"[5] on the rug whenever we were particularly busy; seeming to regard with pitying indulgence the fuss which two-legged creatures made about trifles disconnected with the real concerns of life, namely, sport and dinner. But instead of calling Allah to witness our strange and foolish behavior, our second dog takes the keenest interest in everything we do which he cannot understand — pasting, painting, needlework, using a sewing-machine or a chessboard, lighting a spirit-lamp, arranging a cabinet, — it is all a matter of intensest curiosity to our poor friend, who stands on his hind legs for an agonizing period, and sniffs and looks, and asks us with his eyes, What it all means? And, alas! alas! we cannot tell him. Between his intellect — more full of the wholesome spirit of inquiry than that of half our human pupils — and our own, there is no medium of communication which suffices to let the knowledge he seeks pass from us to him; and so the little eager gaze dies away at last in inevitable disappointment. The same dog who will display such curiosity as this (and I not only "have met," but possess one fairly eaten up with it), will also hunt out in the woods every odd. creature, and study it for half an hour together. Twice my dog has discovered the caterpillars of the goat-moth, and she is constantly to be found seated gravely before a humble-bee, an earthworm, or a slug, deliberately watching its movements, and occasionally (I regret to say) accelerating them by means of a certain sharp experimental scratch with her paw. A railway train, seen for the first time, running across a distant valley, filled her with astonishment; and after ingeniously running round a projecting hill-side, so as to watch it again after it had passed behind it, she came back to me with the question speaking in every gesture, " What *was* that wonderful thing?" For a child of three times her age to display similar thirst for knowledge would be to hold out the promise of a new Humboldt.

Lastly (for this sort of contrast might be drawn out *ad infinitum*), our dogs display their affection towards us in the most curiously-varied. modes. As a rule, dogs, having no language to supplement their caresses, are of course more demonstrative than human beings; but if the master do not respond to the

---

[5] "Kef," a state of dreamy tranquility.

demonstration, the finer-natured dog retreats into himself, and (as is the case with the colleys of most shepherds)[6] lives a life of devotion, and sometimes dies of despair on his master's grave, but never tells his love by so much as a lick of the hand. There are great varieties, also, in the manner in which dogs will display their feelings even to a person who encourages their caresses. There are horrid little pampered beasts who obviously like to be stroked, not as a token of affection, but because it pleasantly rubs their tight skins, and who would as soon be shampooed by a hairdresser as caressed by their foolish mistress. When the stroking ceases they turn round imperiously, "Go on, I say," and scratch viciously till the process be renewed, or they are turned out of the room. The dog who really loves his master delights in mere propinquity, likes to lie down on the floor resting against his feet, better than on a cushion a yard away, and, after a warm interchange of caresses for two or three minutes, asks no more, and subsides quietly in perfect contentment. That a short tender touch of the dog's tongue to hand or face corresponds exactly, as an expression of his feelings, to our kisses of affection, there can be no sort of doubt. All dogs kiss the people they love in this way by instinct, and sometimes have curious little individual fancies about the way they do it. My own dog, as a tiny puppy, took a fancy thus to kiss or bite my ear; and being stolen and lost for nine weeks while too young dearly to remember me, this propensity enabled me to identify her most satisfactorily on her restoration.

Of course the return of a master after absence is the crucial occasion in which a dog's love is displayed. It is impossible for us, who so rarely embark our whole heart's longings in a single affection, and who receive news by every mail from absent dear ones, to conceive the feelings of an animal whose entire being is swallowed up in attachment to his master, and to whom that master's absence is a severance complete as death, and who then, when inevitably wholly unprepared, hears the dear voice and beholds again the form he adores, suddenly restored. If the absence has been long, and the dog's affection of the more concentrated kind, he sometimes dies, like Argus, of the shock, and always he is powerfully affected. A young and lively dog will leap a score of times to kiss his master's face, but an older one will generally cling to him in silent ecstasy, and perhaps suffer serious physical derangement, like a human being who has passed through an over-exciting scene.

Much of the variety apparent in the character of dogs no doubt results from the behavior of their owners. Not only do people reflect their peculiarities on their dogs in a mysterious fashion, but they live with them on wholly different terms and in different relationships. A dog is an idol in one family, a friend in another, a slave

---

[6] Colleys, a reference to the Scotch sheep-dog, also spelled "collie."

in a third. Busy people spare only a moment now and then to bestow a hasty pat on the poor brute who is hungering for affection. Philanthropists mostly treat him with a distant and condescending benevolence, to the last degree offensive to his feelings; and both gushing and misanthropic folks make a fool of him, to his ill-concealed disgust, by lavishing more endearments than he cares to return. In some houses an absolute despotism is the established form of government, the dog is allowed no *motu proprio* whatever,[7] and discipline is enforced by terrible penalties, of which it is dreadful to speak. Other people live with their dogs in a republican manner, or what the *Vril Ya* would call a "Koom Posh,"[8] and the dog does that which is pleasant in his own eyes, and generally unpleasant in those of unfortunate visitors. In such cases the owner of the animal is merely considered in the light of a well-intentioned officer of state, appointed to attend to the commissariat and other matters connected with the dog's comfort and. well-being. If he fulfil his duty, well and good; the dog will be pleased graciously to accept the attentions offered. If he neglect it, then the ill-used quadruped will "know the reason why." Undoubtedly both these extremes are evil, and no constitution less beautifully balanced than that of the British Empire can adjust the nice relationships of dogs and men, reserving the rights of all, and securing the greatest happiness of the greatest number. Worst of all are those oligarchies where several of the upper class (as I suppose we must call the men) divide the government. No dog can serve two masters, much less three or four masters and mistresses; and. his proper feelings of allegiance and devotion are all destroyed by placing him in so unnatural a position, analogous only to the polyandry practiced in Thibet. And, on the other hand, for one human being to keep several dogs at once (real pet house-dogs, not poor slaves of the kennel-harem), is a violation of what the Germans would call the root-idea of the relation. When one dog is dead, after a reasonable interval the widowed owner may, without violation of decency, take to himself another canine companion. But polydoggery is a thing against which all proper feeling revolts . . . .

[O]f all the current mistakes about dogs, the most exasperating is the vulgar delusion that, they have no faults, that all their virtues are mere matters of course; and that we may expect every dog to be magnanimous and courageous, as we expect a table to be firm, or a drawer to open and shut. The grand Wattsian aphorism, "It is their nature *to*," exhausts the popular philosophy of the subject, and the meanest cad

---

[7] *Motu proprio*, a document issued by a monarch on his own initiative. Thus, in this situation, the dog is allowed no initiative or leeway in his or her behavior.

[8] "Koom Posh", a form of egalitarian democracy in Edward Bulwer Lytton's utopian novel, *The Coming Race* (1871).

will pat a dog condescendingly on the head for an act of heroism which he could not himself perform to save a drowning universe. To understand how good are dogs, it is absolutely necessary (as Hegel would tell us,) to recognize also their badness. We must see that the "best of dogs has his faults," if we would appreciate the merits which redeem from absolute contempt even the most pusillanimous cur. I have used the word "faults," but I am not sure that we might not equally properly speak of the crimes of dogs, for the turpitude of some of their actions certainly surpasses mere failure in justice or benevolence. There are traitor dogs who have basely accepted bribes of raw meat and remained silent when it was their imperative duty as sentinels to challenge the intruder with the loudest of barks. Moroseness, and even malignity of temper, have betrayed many an animal, otherwise deserving of moral approval, into deeds of violence and murderous attacks on rivals; and the lawless brigandage of others in the matter of their neighbors' bones is almost too common a transgression to be noticed. Even real estate (in kennel property) is disregarded by some marauders, who will hold "adverse possession" against the rightful owner . . . . Others, again, set aside every recognized principle of treaties and friendly alliances.

With endless facts such as these, proving the occasional wickedness of dogs, it is amazing to think how so many people persist in talking of dogs as if their natures were all on a dead level, and it were quite a matter of course that every individual should display all the virtues set down in books of natural history as distinguishing "the dog." Bless their souls! (or whatever does duty for a dog's soul), the dear brutes are a thousand times more lovable and interesting than any such pieces of moral clock-work.

[T]here is always this difference with regard to a dog and a human being, that we see the dog's character *pur et simple*, such as nature made it, whilst we see the man's or woman's through a thick crust of conventionality, and perhaps not once in a year get a glimpse of the real John or Jane behind the veil. When we *do* catch a full sight of a human heart in its anguish or joy, temptation or triumph, of course we love it beyond anything we can feel for a lesser nature. Even when it is a wicked heart, the revelation stirs us to the depth of our being with pity, terror, perchance with a reflection of a lurid light into depths of our own souls. "Nothing human is alien to us." But then it must be the real human passion, not the dreary fiction of a sentiment; — pretense of care for what the speaker cares nothing, of pleasure in what he does not enjoy, of hopes, loves, fears, interests, admirations, all second-hand and half-affected if not absolutely unreal, which make up the staple of social intercourse. Now, with our humble dog, there is none of all this. Everything in him is genuine to the heart's core, and, so far as his nature goes, we reach him at once, and love him at once.

I have said there are dogs capable of ascending to the heights of martyrdom, and surely there are many whose lives are inspired by the purest self-sacrificing love, and who die (in their simple unconscious way) real martyrs to the cruelty of men . . . . How many dogs are there now in the world who forever return blows and ill-treatment with devoted service, and who would in an instant, leap into fire or water to save the man who the moment before had been kicking or scourging them? Of course it is common to slur over all the stories of such magnanimity when it is a dog who has been the hero, with that stupid word "Instinct." But if we analyze what we mean by instinct in such a case we shall find that, if the act loses moral elevation by the absence of deliberative choice, it gains almost as much in lovableness by the simplicity and unconsciousness with which the grand self-sacrifice is achieved. It is not that a dog rushes blindly to death and danger. He knows just as well as a man does the risk he runs, and fears pain, and clings to existence as much as we. But, with him, love and generosity are so overpowering that he has no need to stand debating whether he shall give himself for another. It is the spontaneous wish of his fond heart to do so, and, without one hesitation of self-regardful pity, he performs the act for which saints and heroes fit themselves by a lifetime of virtue.

There are a few men who feel only for themselves. There are many who feel only for their own families and friends. Then come those who feel for their own class, their townsfolk or fellow-countrymen. Of recent years, since the interests of men and women have seemed to be distinguished. from one another, it has become apparent that there are thousands who cannot thoroughly sympathize with the wants, sufferings, and wrongs of the opposite sex. Lastly, the power of feeling for animals, realizing their wants, and making their pains our own, is one which is most irregularly shown by human beings. . . . A rough shepherd's heart may overflow with it, and that of an exquisite fine gentleman and distinguished man of science may be as utterly without it as the nether millstone. One thing, I think, must be clear: till a man has learned to feel for all his sentient fellow-creatures, whether in human or in brutal form, of his own class and sex and country, or of another, he has not yet ascended the first step towards true civilization, nor applied the first lesson from the love of God.

———————————

7

Dogs and the Law [1]
(1896)

Roscoe Pound

Roscoe Pound (1870-1960) was a Nebraska-born and educated
botanist, legal theorist, and active sociologist. He taught at the
University of Nebraska, Northwestern University, and
the University of Chicago. His sociological
acquaintances included Edward A. Ross, George
Elliott Howard, Edith Abbott, and Albion Small,
among others. Pound was called to Harvard in 1910
where he subsequently became Dean of the Law
School, and, near the end of his career, offered
courses in the sociology department. He was a
prolific and influential writer.[2] He founded the
American school of plant ecology.[3] His major works
include: *The Phytogeography of Nebraska* (1898),
The Spirit of the Common Law (1921), *Criminal
Justice in Cleveland* (1922), and the five-volume
Jurisprudence (1959). He developed the American

school of sociological jurisprudence and was for twenty-five years an
active member of the American Sociological Society. Pound's
sociological work is well documented,[4] as are his contributions to

---

[1] This tongue-in-cheek institutional spoof, one of Pound's earliest writings, appeared in *The Green Bag* 8 (April 1896: 172-74).

[2] F.C. Setaro, *A Bibliography of the Writings of Roscoe Pound* (Harvard University Press, 1942); G.P. Strait, *A Bibliography of the Writings of Roscoe Pound, 1940-1960* (Harvard University Law School, 1960).

[3] R.C. Tobey, *Saving the Prairies: The Life Cycle of the Founding School of American Plant Ecology, 1895-1955* (University of California Press, 1981).

[4] M.R. Hill, "Roscoe Pound and American Sociology" (Ph.D. diss., University of Nebraska-Lincoln, 1989); M.R. Hill, "Pound, Roscoe" in *Blackwell Encyclopedia of Sociology,*" ed. by George Ritzer (Blackwell, 2007: 3585-87).

legal theory.[5] The primary deposit of Pound's papers is at the Harvard Law School Library and is available on microfilm. An important secondary collection resides at the Nebraska State Historical Society. As a young scholar, Pound harbored an ambition to publish an article in the *Green Bag*, a legal journal that frequently featured humorous essays about the social institution of law. Here is Pound in top satiric form.

IT SEEMS that the common law only took notice of a mastiff, hound, spaniel, and tumbler. But those days are long since passed. Today courts are compelled to take notice of all sorts and conditions of dogs and all manner of suits arising from their natural delight in barking and biting. The law pertaining to dogs has thus reached considerable bulk, if nothing more, and, considering the increasing number of cases in the reports having dogs for their subject- matter or arising out of the doings of dogs, it is somewhat strange, in this age of textbooks, that no one has produced a "compendious treatise" upon the subject. While the profession is waiting for this treatise, I venture a few observations which may be of use to the learned author and serve to help him in filling that portion of his two volumes (there will be two volumes of course) not taken up by the table of contents and the table of cases cited.

In the first place, a few suggestions as to the title. If possible, the word jurisprudence should find a place in the title. We have Medical jurisprudence, Dental jurisprudence, and others of the sort, and I could never see why an author who thought it worth his while to write on the law pertaining to horses, or on the law applicable to farmers, should omit the opportunity of giving us Equine jurisprudence and Rural jurisprudence. But perhaps the latter phrase, or Agricultural jurisprudence, or any equivalent, might be confusing, as suggestive of justices of the peace. At any rate our author must ponder well before he discards Canine jurisprudence. "Commentaries on Canine jurisprudence,"— how insignificant is "A Treatise on the Law of Dogs" in comparison. A Treatise might possibly be compressed into one volume. Commentaries, never!

Next our author will investigate the historical aspects of the subject. He will examine the laws and customs of the Egyptians, he will quote a few passages from

---

[5] D. Wigdor, *Roscoe Pound* (Greenwood, 1974); N.E.H. Hull, *Roscoe Pound & Karl Llewellyn* (University of Chicago Press, 1997).

the Digest, and, if possible, from the Twelve Tables. *Cave canem* may be cited as a maxim of Roman Law applicable to modern conditions. The barbarous doctrines of the common law which did not make dog-stealing larceny will come in for vigorous invective. A suggestion may be made also by which our author may profit in preparing his historical chapter. We learn from Sir Henry Maine[6] that Canine Jurisprudence had attained such development in old Irish law that a large portion of one of the Brehon Law Tracts is taken up with the law relating to dog-fights and injuries to persons attempting to promote or to put an end to them.

These preliminary matters disposed of, the author will define a dog. He will find it laid down quite generally that a dog is "a thing of value." But this search for judicial definition, for no "modern" text-writer will venture an opinion or definition of his own, will be rewarded much better. The Supreme Court of Indiana,[7] without deciding whether or not dogs are "animals," has ruled that they are "brute creatures and domestic fowls." But note, reader, that the court was construing an act of the legislature, and hence the ordinary meanings of words did not necessarily apply. This decision will go far towards explaining a decision of the Supreme Court of Michigan[8] to the effect that it is no justification for killing a dog that he is found under suspicious circumstances in a hen-house. Surely that is a very proper place for a domestic fowl, if not for all brute creatures.

Our author will also find it laid down that dogs are not persons, and hence that dogs are incapable of being police officers or constables,[9] though animals of less reputed intelligence than the dog have been known to fill higher positions: presumably because they were persons.

Following approved methods of classification, our author will doubtless proceed to consider (1) Rights of Dogs, (2) Duties and Liabilities of Dogs, (3) Duties and Liabilities of Persons Dealing with Dogs. A few suggestions may be made under each head.

A writer has recently given an affirmative answer to the question: "Have animals rights?" and as Austin and others of his close way of thinking, who would scout such a proposition, are growing out of fashion, we may expect our author to maintain through several pages of vigorous rhetoric that dogs have rights, — and therefore that they have legal rights. How these rights are to be enforced is a serious

---

[6] Sir Henry Sumner Maine (1822-1888).

[7] State *v.* Giles, 125 Ind. 154.

[8] Bowers *v.* Horan, 93 Mich. 420.

[9] Heisrodt *v.* Hackett, 3 Cent. Law Journ. 479.

question which the exigencies of argument may require him to leave unanswered. How far masters are to be regarded as the natural guardians of dogs, and whether the rights of canine litigants should be protected by guardians *ad litem* appointed for the purpose, we are not prepared to say.

The duties and liabilities of dogs are everywhere the subject of legislation. To wear collars, to refrain from running at large, and not to amuse themselves by worrying sheep, are universal requirements. But the common law has something to say under this head. In considering the common law duties of dogs, our author will do well to follow Dr. Watts, whose classification of the propensities of dogs seems to have been confirmed judicially. In this way the duties of dogs may be classified under two heads, (1) to abstain from barking, (2) to abstain from biting. For it has been ruled that the tracking up of freshly painted doorsteps by a dog is not actionable.[10] In that case the dog in question was wont to exercise his vocal powers about the premises of the complainant, and in addition to defacing the painted steps invaded the hen-roost, whereupon the owner of the premises brought *quo warranto* with his revolver and executed an ouster. The court ruled that the action did not lie. But *aliter* as to the barking where a dog brought with him divers companions, votaries of Luna, and led a nocturnal chorus.[11] It would seem that it was the unlawful combination and conspiracy which made the barking especially reprehensible in the latter case. The law appears to recognize a distinction between barking and biting, in that, while biting is always unlawful,—at least where the bitee is human, — barking is not *malum in se,* but only becomes reprehensible when accompanied by circumstances of aggravation, such as the combination and conspiracy just noted, or the frightening of a horse, etc. It seems also that the circumstances of aggravation must grow out of or be closely connected with the barking. It is not enough that they merely accompany the barking. An example of this is the defacement of the freshly painted steps noted above. There the injury did not properly arise out of the barking, nor was it in strictness connected therewith. As the courts of Michigan issue injunctions against the use of profanity, even on one's own premises, the case of the owner of the steps in question would seem to be one of *injuria absque damno.*[12]

In discussing the rights and liabilities of persons having to do with dogs, our author will meet with many interesting questions. In the first place, he will find it

---

[10] Bowers *v.* Horan, 93 Mich. 420.

[11] Hubbard *v.* Parsons, 90 Mich. 221.

[12] An injury without legal damage – Eds.

45

laid down that the law has no respect for the characteristics and prejudices of dogs.[13] But this statement must be taken with some qualification, for the same court has held, that it is contributory negligence to pull a dog's tail.[14] On the other hand, it is not contributory negligence to offer candy to a dog, nor to step on a dog in the course of a scuffle with "a third party."[15] Nor is it contributory negligence to take a dog by the collar for the purpose of preserving the peace and rescuing a dog "rightfully in the plaintiff's custody."[16] But the court wisely suggest that a great deal must depend in such cases on the size and disposition of the dogs.

In Massachusetts the county is made liable to owners of sheep for damage done to their sheep by dogs, and the county may recover over from the harborers of the dogs. Under this statute a peculiar case arose where the dog of the owner of the sheep conspired with divers dogs of the defendants to worry his master's sheep, and in pursuance of such conspiracy, aided and abetted by the dogs of the defendants, did kill one or more sheep of his master of great value (of course). The defendants were held liable to the county for the damage, the rule being, apparently, that the cussedness of the dog is not to be imputed to his master so as to preclude a recovery for the damage done by his co-conspirators.[17]

Many other points might be noticed. But I trust enough has been said to indicate the field which lies open for some industrious author and enterprising publisher. The profession will wait impatiently for a Treatise on Canine Jurisprudence. I cannot hope for the honor of a dedication, which will be reserved for some eminent occupant of the bench. May I hope that these suggestions will be rewarded by a presentation copy of the two volumes when issued? I fear not, such is human ingratitude, unless I can outdo the regular writers of testimonials and reviews for circular publication, and furnish the enterprising publisher aforesaid *quid pro quo.*

---

[13] Boulester *v.* Parsons, 161 Mass. 182.

[14] Raymond *v.* Hodgson, 161 Mass. 184.

[15] Lynch *v.* McNally, 73 N.Y. 347; Fake *v.* Addicks, 45 Minn. 37.

[16] Matterson *v.* Strong, 159 Mass. 497.

[17] Worcester *v.* Ashworth, 160 Mass. 186.

8

On Dogs [1]
(1911)

Charlotte Perkins Gilman

Charlotte Perkins Gilman (1860-1935) was a contemporary and friend of Jane Addams, Edward A. Ross and Lester Frank Ward. An active member of the American Sociological Society, she pursued an active career of sociological writing and lecturing outside the academy. She was a prolific writer.[2] Gilman is best known for *Women and Economics* (1898) and is increasingly recognized for her substantive sociological monographs.[3] She wrote, edited and published a journal, *The Forerunner*, from 1909-1916. Her autobiography is *The Living of Charlotte Perkins Gilman* (1935). Concise introductions to her sociological perspective are readily available.[4] Gilman is also the subject of a large body of literary criticism, some of which borders on the bizarre and should be read with great caution.  Gilman's archival papers are at Harvard University in the Schlesinger Library on the History of Women in America (portions of this collection have been digitized and are available online).

---

[1] Edited from *The Forerunner* 2 (1911: 180-82, 206-9).

[2] G. Scharnhorst, *Charlotte Perkins Gilman: A Bibliography* (Scarecrow, 1985).

[3] Eg., *The Dress of Women: A Critical Introduction to the Symbolism and Sociology of Clothing*, ed. by M.R. Hill and M.J. Deegan (Greenwood, 2002) and *Social Ethics: Sociology and the Future of Society*, ed. by M.R. Hill and M.J. Deegan (Praeger, 2004).

[4] M.J. Deegan, "Gilman's Sociological Journey from Herland to Ourland" in Gilman's *With Her in Ourland: Sequel to Herland*, ed. by M. Deegan and M.R. Hill (Greenwood/Praeger, 1997: 1-57); M.J. Deegan and C.W. Podeschi, "The Ecofeminist Pragmatism of Charlotte Perkins Gilman," *Environmental Ethics* 23 (Spring, 2001: 19-36); M.R. Hill, "Gilman, Charlotte Perkins," in *Blackwell Encyclopedia of Sociology*, ed. by George Ritzer (Blackwell, 2007: 1941-42).

I

MAN'S RELATION to the other beasts has been an interesting one from the beginning. According to the Hebraic account, he was created master of all the lower animals, but according to anthropology, he has had a long up hill struggle for supremacy.

In some parts of the world, this supremacy is still maintained by effort, and occasionally open to question — a matter of "suzereignty" rather than dominion. Of our carnivorous competitors, we have exterminated some, or at least outlived them; with some we are still at war in frontier regions; and some have become our friends or servants, as the cat and dog, cow, horse and sheep.

To the milder vegetarian animals we have helped ourselves, literally, using their strength, their covering, their meat and milk as we chose; and modifying them to suit our needs or fancies.

Our most difficult opponents are the smaller creatures, disrespectfully termed vermin; as we have recently seen in New Zealand, where the injudiciously imported rabbit found the country so much to his liking that he took possession by right of numbers, and is said to descend from the hills at certain seasons of the year like a gray blanket. Man has to bestir himself to maintain his supremacy in the presence of so much rabbit as this.

Our first method of dealing with the well established old families of beasts, who naturally resented the appearance among them of the agile and ingenious biped, was simply to kill them — when they did not kill us.

But later on we learned to coerce and use them to our economic advantage, just as we learned to make slaves instead of corpses of our prisoners of war.

We found a wide field and made free therein. From tame elephants to performing fleas; from trick horses to fancy pigeons; from the mild-eyed milk-machine to the hunting leopards of India, man has tried his hand on creatures without number.

With incubators and fish-hatchery he dabbles in the processes of nature; with the careful study of the breeder and the silly experiments of the fancier he distorts or improves the house of life at will.

In and out among the beasts he takes his way, laying a heavy hand on this and a slight touch on that; calling one to sturdy comradeship and another to the hollow cruelty of pet-dom; and others, again, to direct slavery under chain and lash.

Slowly he has risen, dragging his subjects with him, keeping them alive for his own uses, though long since modified out of all direct relation with nature. If the human race died off the earth, many animals would perish with it, and others revert to unrecognizable earlier forms; so absolutely do they depend on us for their existence.

We have literally made certain animals, as the Japanese makes his dwarf trees. Natural processes keep them alive, but we, checking and guiding those processes, have made them what they are.

The mule is one of our manufactures, ill tempered and sterile, no doubt unhappy in his hybrid consciousness, but a useful pulling machine. The gross and filthy hog is another of our masterpieces. Not content with the beast as God made it, we fell to and altered this edible brother to suit an educated taste. He has his revenge on us too, but not the satisfaction of knowing it.

Some day we shall learn more about food and its consequences, and see that the tortured goose of Strasbourg, the degraded pig, and the rest of our victims, have had means of retaliation after all.

In all these conscienceless dealings with living forms, no creature has been more constantly under man's hand than the dog. Their connection is perhaps the earliest of all, dating far back to prehistoric times when there was not so much difference between man and the other brutes.

The hunting savage saw and envied the skill of the hunting dog. The wild dog hunted in packs and so developed the capacity for concerted action, for obedience to signal, and for division of a common victim, which made him more amenable to the new combination than the individualistic feline carnivore.

Cheetah, cormorant, hawk — man succeeded in taming and training many creatures to help him hunt, but the dog was most submissive and most serviceable.

Perhaps it is owing to the jackal ancestry with which our dog is credited, that he took so kindly to restraint and command, cuffs and kicks and curses; and so man grew to love him.

The jackal theory accounts for the presence of the dog most perfectly, for that ingenious beast was always a follower, tagging the lion and tiger for their leftovers of bones and carrion, and when man proved the most successful hunter, he tagged him.

He became a creature useful, faithful, utterly submissive; a helpless unresisting humble slave; a thing upon its back with futile paws all waving in the air — this manner of beast appealed to the spirit of primitive man, and the two were united securely.

The union holds long after the use has ceased; and the dog lingers on in prolonged survival as a well-beloved rudiment. He is grafted upon humanity as a fixture it appears, though his value lessens with the advance of civilization, and his own health, happiness and dignity lessens in the same proportion.

It is easy to account for the prehensile tail, or the fly-flap tail, or the tail of warmth and shelter; but the tail of the cat seems to have no use save as a vehicle of expression; a continuity of nerve action maintained as a sort of relief to the feelings. So the dog, as a human appanage, seems to have no other explanation than an emotional one; he is a vehicle of expression for the larger creature, a relief to the nerves.

His original service was that of hunter and great was his value when hunting was our chief means of support. When hunting becomes merely a sport, we have the dog still "useful" in a process which has no use; a sort of toy for grown men in a game the pleasure of which lies in giving full swing to the instincts and passions of our racial infancy.

These are crude instincts, brutal passions, which the wise freedom of our later life-processes tend steadily to eliminate, but which men still find pleasure in because it is easier to slip downward than to push up. We indulge in make-believe the impulses once respectably useful, and so maintain by artificial aid these remnants of a once stalwart savagery, as we might proudly foster and exhibit a faintly wriggling rudimentary tail.

After the hunting period came the dog's noblest use, in his place as shepherd. To learn to protect his whilom prey, to fight for instead of against a helpless thing, to apply his energy and intelligence to taking care of a creature instead of destroying it, this was splendid progress for the dog.

In this work grew his soul as man's grew under the same influence. He had to use new capacities, higher capacities, and had higher pleasure in them. So from mere foxiness he grew to wisdom, developing a broader intelligence in this complex interaction with man as a caretaker and defender. The herd-dog is a noble and healthy creature; and not distinguished for a spaniel-like servility. He obeys, but does not fawn and cringe so much. He know[s] his power and value.

Then followed long ages of agriculture; and still, on isolated farms, the dog was useful as a guardian, and happy in his usefulness. Free also to some degree, and happy in his freedom. Hunter, shepherd and watch dog, or sled-dog of the snowlands, all these are respectable.

Then comes the city and the pet.

Modern civilization is industrial in its main economic features, though still based on agriculture, and, more remotely, on cattle keeping. As that civilization advances, and villages swell and thicken into cities, the dog has less and less of [an] honest place.

He has not the physical strength for bearing burdens, though so used in Holland, somewhat, and in Northern countries of deep snow. He has not sufficient ingenuity to assist in manufacture; there is nothing to hunt but an occasional cat; no need to watch or defend, for the policeman guards, and the skilled burglar cares little for a dog.

Each living animal has a mechanism developed through ages of exercise to perform certain acts. If prevented from the use of his natural abilities the creature suffers. To supply his wants, and "love" him, is not enough. No live thing can be happy unless it is free to do what it is built for. The more complex and advanced the abilities of an animal, the more he suffers without their use. This is not merely from an unhappy state of mind, but from an interference with physiological processes, sure to invite disease. The dog is the most diseased of animals, next to man, because his life is so unnatural.

In a modern industrial community he has no legitimate activities of his own, and none of ours; on the contrary he holds a position of absolute parasitism, and of more or less injury to us.

The city statutes recognize this and seek to restrict the dog as a nuisance. He has, indeed, become not only useless and expensive, but a positive danger. In seeking to protect ourselves against the dangers incident to dogs in cities, we are forced to add cruel restrictions to canine life.

He must be collared, he must be chained, he must be muzzled, he must not be allowed in the places where he would prefer to go, his life becomes increasingly a burden.

A slave without any industry to justify his slavery; a prisoner, for no fault to warrant his imprisonment; a captive, led in chains and manacled in his one point of contact with life, his means of inquiry, of expression, of defense, of eating, breathing and panting — his poor muzzle — this is the animal we say we love!

Are we honest in this belief? Is it not merely a transmitted habit of mind sliding down from generation to generation through our unoccupied brains, unchecked by any reasonable survey of the position?

The animal is no longer of advantage to us. If he were, he would not be thus heavily and heartlessly restricted. Are we then of such advantage to him as to make up for his visible sufferings?

As a component part of city life the dog is a direct burden, from the economic standpoint. His food is no great item, for the unpleasing habits of the beast make him cheap to feed, and, in some cases, even valuable as a scavenger. This is mainly in the unclean cities of the Orient, and while it is truly a useful service, it does not add to our esteem for the servant. Neither dog nor vulture ranks as high in this line of usefulness as proper sanitary service of man's devising.

The legal machinery involved in regulating the dog as a nuisance requires some expense, as also the veterinary attendance which grows with the growth of our civilization and the dog's disuse.

51

He is also a destructive agent, not only in the ravages of puppyhood, but through his uncleanly habits. All property exposed for sale on the side walk, and this consists often of food supplies, is exposed to injury from dogs, and gets it. The bases of our buildings are defaced and our sidewalks constantly defiled by these poor prisoners of ours; not in the least to their blame, but to be heavily charged against the "love" that robs an animal of its natural freedom; and forming a very considerable addition to our injuries from their presence.

Then comes the list of injuries to life and limb. There are many beautiful stories of dogs defending and saving human life; and these we spread and repeat continually. There are other stories more numerous than we like to admit, of dogs attacking not only men and women, but little children, with varying amount of harm. Unless it is some very tragic case, these hardly reach the newspapers, but personal experience supplies the lack.

The terror of small children from the presence of these large carnivora in our streets is a needless shock to their nervous system. We are used to them and know them to be mainly harmless, but the little child has no such comfort, and is often as much frightened as if the gleaming teeth, face high before him, were those of a lion.

Greatest of all our dangers from dogs is that of hydrophobia, a disease of peculiar horror, to which this friend of man is especially subject; another proof of his jackal ancestry. The skunk also is said to be affected with this disorder and to transmit it by his bite, but as this beast is not commonly domesticated or at large among us, the list of accidents from skunk-bite is not long.

II.

A heavy charge against the dog in cities is the abominable noise he makes. The unmusical love-making or warfare of the cat is a continual grievance, hotly, resented; but one chained dog in a back yard can keep the inhabitants of a block awake, and we endure it patiently.

The noise made by cats is piercing and discordant enough, but it has one merit — the creatures making it are having a good time in their own way, with amorous serenade or taunting war-cry; but the dog's noise has the burden of deep anguish. He is not free on fence or roof, but chained, imprisoned, helpless, cold, alone; he is not a vociferous Lothario, but doomed to endless celibacy; and so he fills the air with howls of woe, to the double distress of powerless listeners. The necessary noises of our cities are sufficient drain on human health without our carefully maintaining these loud unhappy ones.

52

The city dog is not useful but useless, and in varying degrees expensive and injurious. He is not happy — his manifold diseases prove that conclusively. He has sunk from friend, comrade, helper, servant, to the position of a pet, and it is this position which calls for honest examination.

Of what nature is this relation between dog and man? Is it good for him? Is it good for us?

It is easy to answer for the dog. Nature's one silent and ceaseless protest against a wrong position is disease. The dog's relation to man, in cities, is so artificial, so devoid of any legitimate use, so full of painful restrictions, that he responds with a black record of man-made ailments.

In our high-handed seizure of the beast's whole life, we have robbed him of freedom in essential natural processes, condemned him to a universal celibacy, and thus introduced him not only to some of the physical disorders of mankind, but some of our vices, as well. The love of man for dogs is not well proven by this general injury.

Those who are prepared to honestly defend the dog's place in the city will maintain that he is so developed in his power to love mankind that he derives a greater pleasure from our companionship than pain from all his losses and restrictions.

This is only provable by a fair trial. Let us suppose a case — a work of pure imagination necessarily, because the dog is now so far from nature. Suppose some dogs, living freely together, mating and rearing their puppies happily, with plenty of food and water and exercise. Then suppose a dog sufficiently devoted to a man to leave his freedom for a kennel, collar, and leash; to leave his mate and young for loneliness and strained converse with occasional fellow prisoners; to leave the joy of hunting and the savor of fresh game for tossed table scraps; and his natural exercise for the art of standing on his hind legs, or fetching stones. Do we really think he would do it?

This is all nonsense, of course, for the wild dog does not care for man, and the tame dog does not know freedom. Cut off from man today, he is indeed a miserable wretch, were he to leave his master. From pauper he must become a thief; from slave, a fugitive. He loses all and gains nothing but the freedom of cold and starvation. The modern dog is completely parasitic in his relation to man, and the affection which holds him to us runs exactly parallel with his only means of support.

Love can never be fairly measured when it lies close to self interest; however deep, submissive, lasting, it is open to the gravest of suspicions.

Suppose the dog did not love man — was surly, fierce, and of a haughty, retaliatory spirit. He would meet with treatment severely painful, and presently cease to exist.

Watch a stray dog trying to ingratiate himself with a hoped-for master — *i.e.,* feeder and protector. He knows how to place himself with the stronger animal whose care he covets. He is grateful, too, and faithful, sticking staunchly to the hand that feeds him, even if it beats him also. But in spite of all this palpable weight of interest in the love of dogs for man, no one who knows dogs at all can question the sincerity and depth of their devotion.

The power of love developed in the dog by his dependence upon us is something wonderful — a type for man to study.

It may be accounted for in origin on purely economic grounds, but it is there as a fact, nevertheless — a capacity for deep and faithful love in the face of neglect and abuse.

Yet this very capacity is a doubtful benefit to the dog. Love is a pleasure in its rich expression, and in its full return. To love as much as a dog loves and have only a wet tongue and wagging tail to express it with — and to have one's caresses rather disliked by the beloved object, must be something of a cross. Up springs the loving dog, all aflame with devotion — muddy paws on our clothes, sloppy tongue on our faces — and we bear it awhile if we are good-natured, and then tell him to "go lie down!" If not good-natured, we will have none of it.

So long as the dog could express his love in service he was easier; and the old instinct reasserts itself when the prancing creature hurriedly brings to us anything he can pick up — till we tire of it.

It may well be questioned whether the dog's great love does not give him more pain than pleasure when he has no longer any real avenue of expression.

Another element of his distress is in the irritating pressure of the abilities we have so carefully developed in him during his centuries of usefulness, and which find no exercise in his city life. Acting in unison with man so long, he desires in every quivering inch to act so still; and, failing to be used as before, becomes a reservoir of unbalanced energy. He is the engine and man the engineer. He cannot run his own machinery. Hence the nervous, aimless activity when his master takes him out.

In running frenziedly around and around he spends this current of energy which has no right expression; a yelping, quivering streak of enthusiasm, he rushes frantically to bring a stick or stone, to relieve the pent-up forces of his unnatural life.

Unless we allow full expression to the love and the ability we have developed in the dog, he must suffer deeply in his abortive position.

There remains the plea of benefit and pleasure to man — the dog may not like it, but we do. Our gain lies in loving the faithful creature and in enjoying his love. This is so universal a feeling that it requires very conscientious and careful analysis.

How and why do we love dogs?

54

Our love for them is open to condemnation on the spot by its indifference to their comfort, health, and happiness. Do we "love" creatures which we are content to mutilate, enslave, imprison; whose living bodies we desecrate by breeding them to shapes of artificial ugliness — to such physical discords as are surely doomed to various diseases? What manner of love is this?

We cannot love the dog with admiration and honor: indeed, we usually despise him for the very traits we praise. It is a curious paradox, this. We call him "a noble animal," and "the friend of man"; yet our vilest name for lowest enemy is the name of "Dog!" Dog in all its variants — "Cur!" "Puppy!" "Whelp!" and "Hound!" — there is no baser term save one, one which our usage has made even obscene — the name of the poor dog-mother as we have made her.

In what way do we love the dog? Not with the tender, reverent interest of the student of nature's forms — the dog can show us only a tangled mass of mixed traits from our arbitrary cross-breeding and special development; and not with the wise and gentle care which man owes to all his little brothers who are useful to him — if we so loved we could not bear the pathos of those patient eyes.

Our love for dogs is often of the basest. We love to have with us a submissive vehicle for our will, an unresisting recipient of whatever we choose to bestow; and we prize in our weak and selfish hearts the undiscriminating devotion of a beast who takes us at our lowest, and demands nothing — absolutely nothing — in return for his affection.

However cruel, dirty, and degraded a man may be, his dog will love him none the less. We call it "noble" in the dog, but it has not uplifting influence for the man. Slavish devotion is corrupting to the recipient.

An all-forgiving, unexacting love is beneficent when it comes from a superior, as is the mother's love, or in some conceptions of the love of God; but from a base dependent it does not help us, rather leads to contentment in our ignominy.

A love which carries neither reverence nor service is little more than sensual indulgence. We do not revere the dog, and he bestows his adoration on the just and unjust alike. We ask no service of the dog in the modern city, and so far from serving, we variously imperil him.

There remains of our "love" a low-grade residue of selfish expression, usually found in those who are not satisfied in other and more normal lines. A human being who is in satisfactory relation with his own kind; a happy husband or wife; one rich in children and in friends; or one whose heart goes out to the unhappy, the poor, the sick, the criminal — this is not the one who takes a dog to walk in chains.

A happy heart does not need solace in a dog's caresses, does not turn to this affectionate quadruped for "something to love!" And the great sensitive heart which suffers in the pain of others and longs to help and serve, would be too wisely tender to find pleasure in the pitiful, restricted life of a pet dog.

We try to still our faint qualms on this subject by explaining that our "lap-dogs" are so bred to the position that they know no other life nor want it.

This is true, and a more ingenious and unscrupulous piece of human selfishness was never exhibited. We have deliberately manufactured a little love-machine for our own emotional satisfaction. Breeding our helpless victims as we would — not as they would — we have slowly bred out of them all larger, freer instincts and abilities, bred them small — bred them hideous — bred them as fantastic whim desired — merely because this large animal likes to have a little one groveling beside it, the living exponent of his ruthless power.

Veblen, in his "Theory of the Leisure Class," has some plain words on the maintenance of fancy-bred dogs as a form of "conspicuous expenditure," or "conspicuous waste."[5]

To exhibit one's power, one's wealth, one's taste, has always been a pleasure to the underbred human soul; and its meanest form lies in the exhibition of helpless dependents. There was a time when rank and riches delighted to exhibit some poor zany, some defective mind or body, fool, cripple, or dwarf, as a sort of plaything and proof of superiority.

We have advanced far enough in real cultivation to shrink at such a sight today; but we do not shrink as we see the servant leading the Great Dane or St. Bernard — splendid creatures in their natural place and use — but bought and shown by us merely to prove — what? That we can own a thing like that.

Neither do we recoil at the little deformities so carefully developed to please our refined tastes — the Chinese ugliness of the pug, or the bulldog who out-Herods Herod in his "points" till his hair is fairly bred off his body.

There will come a time when a cultivated civilized human being will feel only pain and horror at the distortion of a live animal, either by the simple savagery of mutilation or the more refined, insinuating cruelty of artificial breeding.

The normally cultivated dog is miserable in the aimless, useless life of a mere pet; the dog who is contented to be a pet is the living proof of our esthetic grossness. Moreover, the pet, the lapdog, the creature maintained purely on emotional grounds as a vehicle of "love," is the least noble and the most diseased. As artificially bred, he is weak in constitution, and in his unnatural life he is an easy prey to many maladies.

---

[5] Thorstein Veblen, *The Theory of the Leisure Class: An Economic Study of Institutions* (New York: Macmillan, 1899).

On the pet dog also comes the weight of criminally wasted wealth in dress and decoration. In Paris there are three establishments where human beings labor to make clothes, ornaments, and other articles for dogs. These things are sheer waste of human energy, and constant injury to the poor beasts.

Behind the misused screen of "love" lurks one large reason why the dog gives us pleasure, why we maintain the hapless creature at his expense and ours. He is a tempting vehicle for the human will.

He is not only a sort of live doll to cuddle and punish and decorate as we are casually inclined; but he is also a species of mechanical toy, somewhat more intricate and lasting than a tin one.

The desirable quality in dogs is obedience; absolute unwearying obedience. A good quality when put to a useful end, but put by us today to most absurd and shameful ones. It is a sort of sensuous pleasure to us to dominate and manage; to make things "go"; a relief to nervous pressure. We *like* to ride the horse and row the boat and sail the ship and run the engine; and we have full right to the pleasure of it, so long as the use is good.

But to apply our energies to toys, and to futile paltry ends or no ends at all, is the mark of the child or the fool.

The dog, once so efficient a coadjutor in large uses, has kept his instinct of submission to some degree, and is violently trained into it anew during the period of well-whipped puppyhood. So has man kept his instinct of dominance, and loves to use it, even to no purpose. Therefore we see man use the dog as a living expression of his power, merely because he likes to. It is a cheap satisfaction.

To make a little helpless beast go and do something he does not want to, or get something we have no use for; to teach him most elaborately to make a fool of himself in undignified postures and arbitrary methods of eating; all this is of no value to the dog and no credit to the man.

A relationship of this sort is essentially ignoble. It develops no fine qualities in the dog, as real service does; and it develops most unpleasant ones in the man; the qualities of the bully and the despot — a frivolous, infantile despot at that.

Such very general practice in qualities we ought steadily to strive to outgrow is a retarding influence on our true progress.

The dog helped us upward when he was useful, dignified, comparatively free. He helps us down today, and suffers miserably himself.

There should arise among us as fast as education can spread it, a new sense of the proper restriction of dogs. Not only legal restriction, but a refined moral sense and a genuine love for the creature which would draw the line sharply at his own health and comfort.

Freedom and occupation are the essential conditions of healthy life. Only in the country can dogs have these. And we should never so far forget the animal's natural rights as to keep less than two. No living creature can be fully happy or healthy without right use of all its functions.

And beyond this line of normal exercise and enjoyment no one who dared to say he loved a dog would ever drag him to diseased captivity.

———————

9

Dogs, Pigs, and Cities [1]
(1916)

Charlotte Perkins Gilman

ON A FARM, a widespread open-air place of business, where the purifying sun and wind may rapidly improve conditions, no matter how bad, we may keep pigs.

Pigs are not attractive beasts. They are not beautiful, nor graceful, nor fragrant, nor over-intelligent, nor affectionate, nor amusing. They are considered, by most people, good to eat; hence we keep pigs — on the farm.

But in cities we are not allowed to keep pigs. They are too malodorous, and their habits are such as to make them "a nuisance." Hence, in cities of any degree of advancement, no pigs.

How about dogs?

We keep dogs in cities, thousands upon thousands of dogs. They are not as dirty in their habits as pigs, nor are they as dainty in their habits as cats; but they are still what is termed, in Oriental countries, an "unclean beast." Cats we dislike because of the noise they make; but dogs make a noise too, a harsh unpleasant noise, quite frequently to be heard. We do not mind it so much because we love dogs far more generally than we love cats; but some people object to the one quite as much as to the other.

The dog is a far more dangerous animal than the cat. If cats had to be muzzled and leashed and laboriously taken out to walk in ignominious attendance upon their physiological needs there would be no cats. Such is our affection for the dog that we put up with both the danger and the dirt that we may continue to enjoy his society.

The amount of unpleasantness caused by this amiable animal in a thickly populated portion of a city is not small. Where people live in apartment houses, twenty or more families in one house, twenty or more houses to one block, and they all keep a dog — that makes four hundred dogs to a block! It is not as bad as that, of course; not every family keeps dogs. But they are pretty numerous in the apartment house district, and their lives are not happy ones.

---

[1] Edited from *The Forerunner* 7 (1916): 137-38.

A dog is a swift, strong, well-muscled, active creature. He is built for running, and for all manner of swift gambols. To pen him up in a steam-heated apartment is cruelty to animals. However, such is our love for him that we do not mind being cruel. He may become a mere dragging prisoner on a string; he may gasp mutely in his muzzle; he may become swollen and diseased from overfeeding and lack of air and exercise; he may and does pine in celibacy, and often succumbs to ailments caused by one or more, or all, of these conditions, — but we "love" him still.

If we really loved the dog, and not merely our own pleasure in his honest affect, we should provide a proper place for him to be healthy and happy in — or go dogless.

Dogs do not grow on trees, nor propagate like rabbits in the open. We regulate their numbers, and when we are really more humane we shall have dogs only in the country, where they can be well and happy.

———————————

10

Love My Dog! [1]
(1925)

Annie Marion MacLean

Annie Marion MacLean (1869-1934) was born on St. Peter's Bay on Prince Edward Island (P.E.I.) in Canada. She earned a master's degree (1897) and a doctorate (1900) in sociology from the University of Chicago where she was a student of Albion Small, Charles Henderson, and George Herbert Mead. She became friends to many of the women associated with Jane Addams at Hull House. MacLean taught sociology in several academies, but her most important appointment was in the Extension Department at the University of Chicago from 1903 to 1934. She wrote some seven books, at least eighty-seven articles and essays, and nearly one hundred book reviews, if not more. Her major works include *Wage-Earning Women* (1910) and several articles in the *American Journal of Sociology*. She pioneered a number of specialty areas in Chicago sociology and

its application: in work and occupations, gender, race, class, urban life, and social movements. She was the first Canadian sociologist and published several important analyses of that nation before 1910. She also made significant methodological innovations in ethnography, community studies, feminism, and photography. MacLean's major contributions to sociology have come to light only recently,[2] and her biography has been long neglected.[3] MacLean

---

[1] Edited from *The Forum* (July 1925): 143-45.

[2] E.g., M.J. Deegan, "Annie Marion MacLean," in *Women in Sociology: A Bio-Bibliographical Sourcebook*, ed. by M.J. Deegan (Greenwood, 1991: 280-88); M.J. Deegan, M.R. Hill, and S.L. Wortmann, "Annie Marion MacLean, Feminist Pragmatist and Methodologist," *Journal of Contemporary Ethnography* 38 (December 2009: 655-65); R. Rauty, "Introduzione" in MacLean's *Due settimane nei grandi magazzini; Gle Sweat-shops in estate*, Esplorazioni, No. 11 (Kurumuny,

happily spent her life with several companion dogs and wrote the following essay in *The Forum* as a protest against another essay, by Agnes Repplier,[4] published in an earlier issue of that journal. Repplier characterized both dogs and their allies as emotionally needy. To this, MacLean hotly replied: "Love My Dog!"

PERHAPS, as the brilliant Miss Repplier would have us believe,[5] dog lovers are a vain lot seeking from their canine pets admiration and worship, but they are so wedded to their idols they may as well be let alone. It is out of that experience that I speak, for if there is any one subsidiary interest that looms larger than another in my own life, it is pups; they are my pleasure specialty, and as against the Fireside Sphinx I am ready to let them defend themselves. My own dogs have contributed so much in the way of companionship and interest that I am constrained to marshal them in a procession through the years that their charms may captivate others.

My first dog came to me when I was five, a fuzzy little mongrel pup named Prince, who was my loyal playmate for a time. In memory I see a child running against the wind with streaming curls, a naughty Prince at her heels, jumping up, and tearing flying frills and shaking rags in glee. Then he would bury a shoe, or breakfast on a hat and look as wise as anything. Those were happy days when clothes were gaily sacrificed to make a puppy's holiday.

2011).

[3] This lacuna was filled recently by Mary Jo Deegan, *Annie Marion MacLean and the Chicago Schools of Sociology, 1894-1934* (Transaction Publishers, 2014).

[4] Repplier (1855-1950) was an American essayist and biographer. The major biographical statements are E. Repplier Witmer, *Agnes Repplier: A Memoir* (Dorrance, 1957); C.E. Breed, *Agnes Repplier, American Essayist* (Ph.D. diss., University of Michigan, 1994); and J. Lukacs, "Editor's Introduction," *American Austen: The Forgotten Writing of Agnes Repplier* (ISI Books, 2009: 1-60). Agnes Repplier's papers are housed in the Rare Book and Manuscript Library at the University of Pennsylvania.

[5] Agnes Repplier, "The Idolatrous Dog." *The Forum* 71 (February 1924): 181-90.

The next dog was a partnership affair, and I seem to see three children fondling him at once; and he led them a merry chase, always with a dishcloth or some other domestic necessity in his teeth. He was a fox terrier, with a bar sinister. Like another beloved member of the dog family immortalized by Richard Harding Davis, his mother was a black and tan.[6] But what is a pedigreed pup to children? We made him a Prince in memory of the other one, for that was in the days before royalty was in a bad way, and it was held no dishonor to have titles in the family. The Boy among us claimed him, a bit of masculine assertiveness which the girls condoned. Oh! those days of flying feet, with Princie prancing along! We were rushing headlong to the future with never a thought but for the present; and there was no past for us.

MacLean and "Jack"

The third dog was the Boy's and only mine by proxy, but how I loved him! Jack was a retriever, big, strong, and full of pranks. Often when the children's bed time came he would steal a march on the elders by galloping up the back stairs and secreting himself under a bed, hoping with all his dog's heart that he would pass unnoticed, as he sometimes did. And then the frolics that followed as he raced from one room to another! We fondly imagined that we put that over on the elders because they did not always call to us in stern tones! A big capering creature and three children over ten, tiptoeing around trying, rather unsuccessfully I now imagine, to suppress their snickers must have called forth quiet mirth below in the room with all the books where the elders sat.

Jack was the kindest creature imaginable; his temper was always under control which was more than could be said of ours; and he was obedient.

---

[6] Richard H. Davis (1864-1916), author of *Bar Sinister*, a short, sentimental dog story, told from the perspective of a streetwise bull-terrier of "mixed" parentage. The 1903 edition, with illustrations by E.M. Ashe, is particularly charming.

Since comparisons are odious, I shall not compare our obedience with his. I see Jack now standing wistfully at the gate when the Boy went off to school, eager — so eager to go, but staying there because he was not invited to accompany his master. When it was time for the Boy to return, Jack would station himself on top of a big square gate post where he could view the street for half a mile, and he could not be diverted from his watching. When he glimpsed his beloved, his excitement and joy were intense; he would almost wag himself off the post, but he would never offer to get down till he heard a childish whistle in the distance. Then he became a study in one dimension as he hurtled himself through the intervening space.

Once our hearts were very sad for Jack was lured away by a thieving vagabond. A week later he found his way back with a broken rope around his neck, tired and dejected looking, yet even then showing his spirit by wanly wagging his tail. He had evidently met hardships on the way. His head was bristling with porcupine quills, mute testimony to sad encounter with one of those little beasties of the woods that shoot their natural arrows at a foe. The Boy and the girls received him into their arms and hearts, and proceeded to extract those quills that hurt him.

The pet of my maturer years was christened Jack in memory of our beloved playmate of earlier days. My Jack was an Irish Setter with never a taint of Sinn Fein about him. Once a man of colossal ignorance caressed him as an English bull, and Jack bravely wagged his tail. He was six months old when he came to me; and a beautiful, wild, leggy thing he was. My wishes were as unheeded as the blowing wind. My come-hither tone was quite likely to send him chasing the whirlwind. On leash, he dragged me around bravely without particular dignity for me.

Fanciers told me that the whip alone could tame a dog, and offered me various styles, but I was always a coward in discipline, and could no more administer corporal punishment to a living creature than I could put a worm on a hook. I was not endowed with heroism for either task. Therefore, I loftily told my critics to wait, and they would see what they would see. Up in the foothills of the Berkshires in summer I put my theories into practice, and proudly returned to Gotham in the fall with a setter at my heels. I had brought this to pass by a system of rewards for good deeds instead of punishments for lapses, and mine was the hand that fed him. Moreover, I never made him a promise I did not fulfil, and I never neglected him. Thus did I train a dear companion who went with me everywhere, and was a great favorite. My training did not make him a slave; there was no servility in him; his obedience was not abject. Once in a hundred times or thereabouts he would assert his personality, and instead of coming at my call, would look speculatively at me, and take a wild free run before returning. This was his privilege. No one creature owes absolute obedience to another.

In childhood, our dogs are only playmates; in maturity, they are friends and teachers. Nature made my setter to run over the stubble and through the marshes after the birds, fate placed him in a lady's boudoir, and he made his adaptation with surprising poise, and surpassing grace. I learned from him that it is possible to be happy in leash, an achievement rare in human beings. But my joy in Jack was not all in philosophizing about his virtues. He made my journeyings to and fro a series of circus performances. On a shopping tour once he jumped nimbly as a chamois to a veil counter and by waving his plumed tail, decorated himself with filmy laces, to the merriment of everyone except the usher who doubtless regarded me as shoplifter. Once on a commuters' train while Jack was sitting proudly beside me, I bade him give his seat to a standing lady. He promptly did so, then leaped lightly to her lap!

Jack was a sportive creature, particularly when he saw his hereditary feline foe. Like a catapult he would shoot through space after pussy. And I have seen elderly, dignified gentlemen revert to type and furtively open an area gate to speed him on his way. This was his one dissipation. One day an irate mother cat, black and with fiery eyes, leaped upon his back and rode him for a block. When she alighted, he sought me in deep contrition, and I had hopes for his reformation. For a week, he took the other side of the street when he saw a *black* cat. Experience seems to be a much overrated teacher!

I well remember the day my setter accompanied me to an important committee meeting where personages sat. He lay at my feet sleeping away the boresome hour till his dogship could stand it no longer. Then, while a pompous gentleman was airing his stupid views on a stupid public question, he arose to his full height, opened his jaws to their widest extent, and emitted a long, loud yawn. He was so pleased by the attention he received that he offered a forgiving paw to the vanquished orator.

This flight of memory calls up many a touching illustration of my dog's devotion. Stricken with illness one day, I was carried away while he was out walking with an admirer. He refused to be comforted, and night after night pulled the clothes from my bed in vain search for his beloved. Finally, he was taken to visit me at the hospital, and, having found me, never again unmade the bed. He slept on it. Looking back I am convinced that a good dog is worth infinitely more than the care bestowed on him and considerate care is essential to the making of a good dog. My Jack was with me five years when he was done to death by a brute in the form of a man who held it no crime to poison a pet. And oh! how the death of a dog can tear a human heart!

Another dog I lately shared with the Boy's boys, Sir Douglas Haig, was an Airedale of high degree, and although never elevated to the peerage, always accompanied me home in lordly fashion. At other times he was a frisky pup, racing with little children and jumping at clothes on a line. I know that shirts and shoes are among the serious matters of life and not to be treated jocosely by pups. Yet to see these things chewed to ribbons and trailed in the dust by a frisky young dog fills my unregenerate soul with glee, a sheer delight that any creature can be so frivolous and happy in a world on the brink of ruin.

These are the dogs who accompanied me through bygone years; they are now where all good dogs go, and my heart gives a thump of sadness as I say it. But there are two others to comfort me. There is Yorrick, Great Dane, king of his kind, huge, beautifully formed, benevolent, an outdoor dog who loves the fireside. And there is the wee, Pekinese pup, Calvin, whose name is redolent of theology and politics, but he cares for neither, satisfied to know that whither I go he will go, content to chase a ball while monarchies and reputations fall.

———————————

11

Dogs and the Conversation of Gestures [1]
(1934)

George Herbert Mead

George Herbert Mead (1863-1931) was born in South Hadley, Massachusetts, to intellectual parents. He entered Oberlin College's Preparatory department in 1876 and matriculated as a freshman at Oberlin College in 1879 where he graduated in 1883. He enrolled in graduate work at Harvard University and in Germany at Leipzig and Berlin. For many years Mead offered a required course in Advanced Social Psychology to sociology students at the University of Chicago. In Chicago, Mead's colleagues included the likes of Edith and Grace Abbott, Jane Addams, Charles Henderson, Mary McDowell, Albion Small, and James H. Tufts. Notable students included Herbert Blumer, Ernst W. Burgess, Ellsworth Faris, Annie Marion MacLean, and William I. Thomas, among others. Mead's innovative ideas, called Chicago pragmatism or

symbolic interactionism, resulted in a flexible model of human behavior where people learn and create meaning through social interaction. One of his most important concepts is "the self" which refers to the ability of a person to become a social object that emerges from the social interaction between the person and the other over time.

It is a long held myth that Mead wrote and published little, but this is only in comparison to the truly herculean output of John Dewey, the man who inadvertently started the myth. The working

---

[1]Edited and excerpted with permission from *Mind, Self & Society from the Standpoint of a Social Behaviorist*, by George Herbert Mead, edited, with introduction by Charles W. Morris (University of Chicago Press, 1934). Copyright 1934 by the University of Chicago. All rights reserved.

bibliographies of Mead's articles in journals are robust, and new books based on Mead's previously unpublished manuscripts continue to appear at regular intervals.[2] Scholarly writing on Mead by sociologists and philosophers is a healthy academic industry.

Mead studied animal and human behavior, or comparative psychology, in Leipzig, under Wilhelm Wundt during the winter of 1888–1889. As a result, Mead believed human behavior was qualitatively different from animal behavior, conceptualizing the processes of symbolization, reflection, meaning, and choice as uniquely human. In the selection below, Mead discusses a dog's behavior as considerably less complex and thoughtful than a human's. Readers are strongly encouraged to consult the full text of Mead's work for the wider context of these passages and the special definitions of technical terms such as "act," "attitude," "behaviorist," "character,""gesture," "social," "stimulus," "symbol," and so on.

An apocryphal story is told on the University of Chicago campus to the effect that Mead was often seen riding his bicycle to and from classes, and that his small dog regularly trotted cheerfully along behind, waited for Mead to finish giving lectures, and then dutifully followed him home again. It is this dog to which Leslie Irvine recently suggested that Mead should have paid more attention.[3] Readers who carefully observe their own dog's behaviors are invited to join Irvine in asking, did Mead get it right?

Mead's papers are found in the Special Collections Research Center at the University of Chicago. Four posthumous volumes of Mead's works were published directly after his death, including *The Philosophy of the Present* (1932), *Movements of Thought in the Nineteenth Century* (1936), and *The Philosophy of the Act* (1938).

---

[2] E.g., G.H. Mead, *The Individual and the Social Self,* ed. by D.L. Miller (University of Chicago Press, 1982); G.H. Mead, *Play, School and Society*, ed. by M.J. Deegan York: (Peter Lang, 1999); Mead, *Essays in Social Psychology*, ed. by M.J. Deegan (Transaction, 2001); M.J. Deegan, *Self, War, and Society: George Herbert Mead's Macrosociology* (Transaction, 2008). A recent careful study of Mead's work as a whole is Daniel R, Huebner, *Becoming Mead: The Social Process of Academic Knowledge* (University of Chicago Press, 2014).

[3] L. Irvine, "George's Bulldog: What Mead's Canine Companion Could Have Told Him about the Self," *Sociological Origins* 3 (Autumn 2003: 46-49); L. Irvine, *If You Tame Me: Understanding Our Connection with Animals* (Temple University Press, 2004).

The selection below is from the most important of these works, *Mind, Self and Society* (1934).

———————————

THE PECULIAR FIELD of social science with which we are concerned is one which was opened up through the work of Darwin[4] and the more elaborate presentation of Wundt.[5]

If we take Wundt's parallelistic statement we get a point of view from which we can approach the problem of social experience. Wundt undertook to show the parallelism between what goes on in the body as represented by processes of the central nervous system, and what goes on in those experiences which the individual recognizes as his own. He had to find that which was common to these two fields — what in the psychical experience could be referred to in physical terms.

Wundt isolated a very valuable conception of the gesture as that which becomes later a symbol, but which is to be found in its earlier stages as a part of a social act. It is that part of the social act which serves as a stimulus to other forms involved in the same social act. I have given the illustration of the dog-fight as a method of presenting the gesture. The act of each dog becomes the stimulus to the other dog for his response. There is then a relationship between these two; and as the act is responded to by the other dog, it, in turn, undergoes change. The very fact that the dog is ready to attack another becomes a stimulus to the other dog to change his own position or his own attitude. He has no sooner done this than the change of attitude in the second dog in turn causes the first dog to change his attitude. We have here a conversation of gestures. They are not, however, gestures in the sense that they are significant. We do not assume that the dog says to himself, "If the animal comes from this direction he is going to spring at my throat and I will turn in such a way." What does take place is an actual change in his own position due to the direction of the approach of the other dog.

We find a similar situation in boxing and fencing, as in the feint and the parry that is initiated on the part of the other. And then the first one of the two in turn changes his attack; there may be considerable play back and forth before actually a

———————————

[4] See: chapter 3, above, this volume.

[5] *Mind, Self & Society*, pp. 42-43. For details and discussion of Wilhelm Wundt's early influence, see: M.J. Deegan, "Introduction: George Herbert Mead's First Book,"*Essays in Social Psychology* by G.H. Mead, ed. by M.J. Deegan (Transaction, 2001: xi-xliv).

stroke results. This is the same situation as in the dog-fight. If the individual is successful a great deal of his attack and defense must be not considered, it must take place immediately. He must adjust himself "instinctively" to the attitude of the other individual. He may, of course, think it out. He may deliberately feint in order to open up a place of attack. But a great deal has to be without deliberation.

In this case we have a situation in which certain parts of the act become a stimulus to the other form to adjust itself to those responses; and that adjustment in turn becomes a stimulus to the first form to change his own act and start a different one. There are a series of attitudes, movements, on the part of these forms which belong to the beginnings of acts that are the stimuli for the responses that take place. The beginning of a response becomes the stimulus to the first form to change his attitude, to adopt a different act. The term "gesture" may be identified with these beginnings of social acts which are stimuli for the response of other forms. Darwin was interested in such gestures because they expressed emotions, and he dealt with them very largely as if this were their sole faction. He looked at them as serving the function with reference to the other forms which they served with reference to his own observation. The gestures expressed emotions of the animal to Darwin; he saw in the attitude of the dog the joy with which he accompanied his master in taking a walk. And he left his treatment of the gestures largely in these terms . . . .

In Wundt's doctrine, the parallelism between the gesture and the emotion or the intellectual attitude of the individual, makes it possible to set up a like parallelism in the other individual.[6] The gesture calls out a gesture in the other form which will arouse or call out the same emotional attitude and the same idea. When this has taken place the individuals have begun to talk to each other. What I referred to before was a conversation of gestures which did not involve significant symbols or gestures. The dogs are not talking to each other; there are no ideas in the minds of the dogs; nor do we assume that the dog is trying to convey an idea to the other dog. But if the gesture, in the case of the human individual, has parallel to it a certain psychical state which is the idea of what the person is going to do, and if this gesture calls out a like gesture in the other individual and calls out a similar idea, then it becomes a significant gesture. It stands for the ideas in the minds of both of them . . . .

To illustrate this further let us go back to the conversation of gestures in the dog-fight.[7] There the stimulus which one dog gets from the other is to a response which is different from the response of the stimulating form. One dog is attacking the other, and is ready to spring at the other dog's throat; the reply on the part of the

---

[6] *Mind, Self & Society*, p. 48.

[7] *Ibid.*, p. 63.

70

second dog is to change its position, perhaps to spring at the throat of the first dog. There is a conversation of gestures, a reciprocal shifting of the dogs' positions and attitudes. In such a process there would be no mechanism for imitation. One dog does not imitate the other. The second dog assumes a different attitude to avoid the spring of the first dog. The stimulus in the attitude of one dog is not to call out the response in itself that it calls out in the other. The first dog is influenced by its own attitude, but it is simply carrying out the process of a prepared spring, so that the influence on the dog is simply in reinforcing the process which is going on. It is not a stimulus to the dog to take the attitude of the other dog . . . .

Animals of a type lower than man respond to certain characters with a nicety that is beyond human capacity, such as odor in the case of a dog.[8] But it would be beyond the capacity of a dog to indicate to another dog what the odor was. Another dog could not be sent out by the first dog to pick out this odor. A man may tell how to identify another man. He can indicate what the characters are that will bring about a certain response. That ability absolutely distinguishes the intelligence of such a reflective being as man from that of the lower animals, however intelligent they may be. We generally say that man is a rational animal and lower animals are not. What I wanted to show, at least in terms of behavioristic psychology, is that what we have in mind in this distinction is the indication of those characters which lead to the sort of response which we give to an object. Pointing out the characters which lead to the response is precisely that which distinguishes a detective office that sends out a man, from a bloodhound which runs down a man. Here are two types of intelligence, each one specialized; the detective could not do what the bloodhound does and the bloodhound could not do what the detective does. Now, the intelligence of the detective over the intelligence of the bloodhound lies in this capacity to indicate what the particular characters are which will call out his response . . . .

What is there in conduct that makes the level of experience possible, this selection of certain characters with their relationship to other characters and to the responses which these call out?[9] My own answer, it is clear, is in terms of such a set of symbols as arise in our social conduct, in the conversation of gestures — in a word, in terms of language. When we get into conduct these symbols which indicate certain characters and their relationship to things and to responses, they enable us to pick out these characters and hold them insofar as they determine our conduct.

A man walking across country comes upon a chasm which he cannot jump. He wants to go ahead but the chasm prevents this tendency from being carried out.

---

[8] *Ibid.*, pp. 92-93.

[9] *Ibid.*, pp. 122-23.

71

In that kind of situation there arises a sensitivity to all sorts of characters which he has not noticed before. When he stops, mind, we say, is freed. He does not simply look for the indication of the path going ahead. The dog and the man would both try to find a point where they could cross. But what the man could do that the dog could not would be to note that the sides of the chasm seem to be approaching each other in one direction. He picks out the best places to try, and that approach which he indicates to himself determines the way in which he is going to go. If the dog saw at a distance a narrow place he would run to it, but probably he would not be affected by the gradual approach which the human individual symbolically could indicate to himself.

About the Editors —

MARY JO DEEGAN and MICHAEL R. HILL have been life-partners since 1982.[1] Together, they have been companions to three wonderful dogs: "Emma Goldman" (a cockapoo),[2] "Charlotte Perkins Gilman" (a Labrador retriever)[3], and, currently, "Annie Marion MacLean" (a Jack Russell terrier). After many years in Nebraska, they now live and work in southwest Michigan.

Emma

Annie

Charlotte

Mary Jo and Michael

---

[1] Mary Jo Deegan and Michael R. Hill, "We're Partners – Not Husband and Wife." Pp. 246-47 in Mary Ann Lamanna and Agnes Riedmann, *Marriages and Families: Making Choices and Facing Change*, 3rd edition (Wadsworth, 1988).

[2] Emma's extraordinary capacity for inventing complicated games was demonstrated in a whimsical yet pointedly didactic essay: Emma Goldman, "Rules for the Game of Bedball," as interpreted by her human companions, Mary Jo Deegan and Michael R. Hill, pp. 7-9 in M. R. Hill, *Principles of Sociology*, Part II (Department of Sociology, Indiana University South Bend, 2004).

[3] Our late Labrador's friendly zest for life was joyfully depicted in an illustrated book for youngsters: Charlotte Perkins Gilman (a Labrador retriever), *Charlotte Looks for Maxine*, as told to Michael R. Hill with advice from Mary Jo Deegan (privately printed, 2006).

MARY JO DEEGAN, born in 1946, earned her Ph.D. in sociology at the University of Chicago (1975). She is Professor Emerita of sociology in the University of Nebraska-Lincoln where she taught for 40 years. Mary Jo is currently Director of the Jane Addams Research Center in St. Joseph, Michigan. Her specialties include the sociology of disability, the sociology of women, and the history of sociology. As an avid collector, Mary Jo is personally and professionally intrigued by canine imagery in costume jewelry.[4] She is the author/editor/co-editor of eighteen scholarly books and numerous articles. Mary Jo won the ASA/HOS Distinguished Scholarly Publication/Book Award in 2003, 2005, 2008 and 2009. Professor Deegan was honored with the ASA/HOS Distinguished Scholarly Career Award in 2002 and, in 2008, with the ASA Peace, War, and Social Conflict section's Robin M. Williams, Jr., Award for Distinguished Contributions to Scholarship, Teaching, and Service.

MICHAEL R. HILL, born in 1944, earned Ph.D. degrees in geography (1982) and sociology (1989) at the University of Nebraska-Lincoln and eventually became a senior tutor in the UNL Department of Athletics. His former teaching posts include: Iowa State University, Albion College, University of Minnesota Duluth, University of Indiana South Bend, Iowa Western Community College, University of Nebraska at Omaha, University of Nebraska-Lincoln, and the University of Notre Dame. As the founder and current editor of *Sociological Origins*, he is deeply interested in the history and development of sociology as an intellectual enterprise. He is the author/editor/co-editor of eleven scholarly books and numerous articles. Michael is now a writer/researcher at D&H Sociologists in St. Joseph, Michigan, where he is also a volunteer docent in the K-12 Understanding Art Program at the Krasl Art Center. Hill has twice won the American Sociological Association (ASA), Section on the History of Sociology (HOS), Distinguished Scholarly Book Award, in 2002 and 2005. In 2003, Dr. Hill was honored with the ASA/HOS Distinguished Scholarly Career Award.

-----

[4] Mary Jo Deegan, "Dog Jewelry" *Sociological Origins* 3 (Autumn 2003: 50-52).

Karen Westendorf online ABEbooks
Also, June 2021